W9-AAC-457

LIGHT ON THE EPISTLES

a reader's guide

by John L. McKenzie

John L. McKenzie Reprint Series

(in order of original publishing)

The Two-Edged Sword

Myths and Realities: Studies in Biblical Theology

The Power and the Wisdom

Mastering the Meaning of the Bible

Authority in the Church

Second Isaiah (Commentary)

The Gospel According to Matthew (Commentary)

Did I Say That?

Light on the Epistles

Light on the Gospels

Theology of the Old Testament

The Old Testament Without Illusions

Source (on contemporary issues)

How Relevant is the Bible?

The New Testament Without Illusions

The Civilization of Christianity

LIGHT ON THE EPISTLES

a reader's guide

by John L. McKenzie

WIPF & STOCK · Eugene, Oregon

Wipf and Stock Publishers
199 W 8th Ave, Suite 3
Eugene, OR 97401

Light on the Epistles
A Reader's Guide
By McKenzie, John L.

ISBN 13: 978-1-60608-045-0
Publication date 12/10/2008
Previously published by The Thomas More Press, 1975

The material in this book appeared
in another form in the newsletter
SEEK 2: A Contemporary Guide to the Epistles

Series Foreword

Mark Twain once ruminated, "It ain't the parts of the Bible I can't understand that bother me; it's the parts I do." John L. McKenzie, commenting on the same subject from another perspective, wrote, "The simple see at once that the way of Jesus is very hard to do, but easy to understand. It takes real cleverness and sophisticated intelligence to find ways to evade and distort the clear meaning of what Jesus said."

But McKenzie, like Twain, was himself a person of exceedingly high intelligence, distinctively witty, with a double-edged sword's incisiveness. As the first Catholic elected President of the Society of Biblical Literature, President of the Catholic Biblical Association, fluent in ten languages, sole author of a 900,000-word Bible dictionary, of over a dozen books and hundreds of essays, John McKenzie attained worldwide recognition as the dean of Catholic biblical scholars.

But again like Twain, McKenzie possessed a cultivated reservoir of abiding empathy—cognitive and emotional—for ordinary people and what they endure, millennia-in and millennia-out. He insisted: "I am a human being before I am a theologian." Unlike many who become entrenched in a hermetic, scholarly world of ever-multiplying abstractions, McKenzie never permitted his God-given faculty of empathy to atrophy. To the contrary, he refused to leave his fellow human beings out in the cold on the doorstep of some empathically-defective theological house of cards. This refusal made all the difference. It also often cost him the support, or engendered the hostility, of his ecclesiastical and academic associates and institutional superiors—as so often happens in scholarly, commercial and governmental endeavors, when unwanted truth that is the fruit of unauthorized empathy is factored into the equation.

John McKenzie produced works of biblically "prophetic scholarship" unlike anything created in the twentieth century by any scholar of his stature. They validate, with fastidious erudition, what the "simple see at once" as the truth of Jesus—e.g., "No reader of the New Testament, simple or sophisticated, can retain any doubt of Jesus' position toward violence directed to persons, individual or collective; he rejected it totally"—but which pastors and professors entrenched in ecclesiastical nationalism and/or organizational survivalism have chronically obscured or disparaged.

In literate societies, power-elites know that to preemptively or remedially justify the evil and cruelty they execute, their think-tanks must include theologians as part of their mercenary army of academics. These well-endowed, but empathically underdeveloped, theological hired guns then proselytize bishops, clergy, and Christians in general by gilding the illogical with coats of scholarly circumlocutions so thick that the opposite of what Jesus said appears to be Gospel truth. The intent of this learned legerdemain is the manufacturing of a faux consensus fidei to justify, in Jesus' sacred name, everything necessary to protect and augment an odious—local, planetary and/or ecclesial—status quo.

John McKenzie is the antidote to such secular and ecclesial think-tank pseudo-evangelization. Truths Jesus taught—that the simple see at once and that Christian Churches and their leaders have long since abandoned, but must again come to see if they are to honestly proclaim and live the Gospel—are given superior scholarly exposition via McKenzie. This is what moved Dorothy Day to write in her diary on April 14, 1968, "Up at 5:00 and reading The Power and the Wisdom. I thank God for sending me men with such insights as Fr. McKenzie."

For those familiar with McKenzie this re-publication of his writings offers an opportunity to encounter again a consistent scholarly-empathic frame of consciousness about Genesis through Revelation, whose major crux interpretum is the Servant of Yahweh (Isaiah 42). Ultimately embodied in the person of Jesus, the Servant is the revealer of Abba almighty—who is "on our side," if our means each person and all humanity. For all Christians, John L. McKenzie's prophetic scholarship offers a wellspring of Jesus-sourced truth about the life they have been chosen to live, the world in which they live, and the Christ in whom they "live and move and have their being."

(Rev.) Emmanuel Charles McCarthy
September 2008
Brockton, Massachusetts

CONTENTS

PREFACE

The history of reading guides to the Bible is nearly as old as the Bible itself; and the success of reading guides is not of a character to encourage one to undertake the task. On any one of the Gospels, commentaries of 600 pages have been written. Most readers find such works not guides but jungles. Anything of a lesser magnitude attempts to answer not all the questions (which is the ideal of the commentator) but those questions which he thinks his reader is going to ask. No author of reading guides has ever been really good at guessing what questions his readers are going to ask. Nor can he cope with the fact that a question asked and answered raises another question which would not have been asked if we had left the whole thing alone.

Yet guides are written and read, probably in the vain hope held by many that there is or ought to be a brief exposition which will answer all their questions instead of raising new ones. This guide will not do that, but neither will any other. It is written with the hope of stating in general what each Epistle is and means to say, and of stating briefly the main point, and only the main point, expressed in successive passages. It is so brief that it may at times be more obscure than the Epistles themselves, which are not as obscure as they are often made out to be. "He who loves his neighbor has fulfilled the law," may be incredible, but it is altogether easy to apprehend. The guide will not make it less incredible, nor can the guide make it easier to apprehend; it may, however, be able to construct a context in which the reader learns that the wisdom of God is the folly of men.

The key to understanding the Epistles is to read them carefully and inquisitively, then reread them, and reread them. . . . Ultimately, every professional scholar makes this his habit. I hesitate to add that even for the scholar this is a reading from faith to faith, but it is. And the individual reader has his own faith, which no one but God can give him. In the community of faith in which the reader and the writer both live, the faith of both can grow by exchange.

John L. McKenzie

Note: At several points in the text I have used the initials JB to indicate *The Jerusalem Bible* and OT or NT for the Old and New Testaments.

Chapter One
INTRODUCTION TO THE EPISTLES

Of the twenty-seven books of the New Testament twenty-one are epistles. This leaves the four Gospels, the Acts of the Apostles and the Revelation of John. But even the Revelation is given the external form of an epistle since it is addressed to the seven churches of Asia. This is not pursued in the rest of the book and there is no epistolary conclusion. The sheer bulk of the epistles makes them highly important; and it is of interest to ascertain, as far as we can, why this was the prevailing form of Christian literature in the apostolic church.

Since the writings of Adolf Deissmann (in German, 1908; revised, 1921), New Testament interpreters are accustomed to emphasize the distinction between the letter and the epistle. Deissmann pointed out that the letter is not literature; it is intended to be read by no one but the addressee, and it is concerned with matters which of themselves are of interest to no one but the writer and the recipient. It is a personal communication, where "literature" is written for anyone who is able and willing to read it. The letter may become literature if the persons involved and the topic of the letter are of general interest, but it was still not written for the general public. This distinction remains even if the letter is addressed to a group such as the church of Corinth and not to an individual or a family.

The epistle was a literary form known in Greek and Roman literature. It was addressed to an individual, usually a friend or a patron of the writer, and it could be written in prose or in verse. Actually it was what we call an essay and was intended for public circulation. The epistles which have survived were produced by literary figures of the ancient world. The epistle can be compared, although not exactly, to the modern letter to the editor. Sometimes the writer does wish to communicate with the editor, but his real and recognized purpose is to state a fact or an opinion to the readers of the journal.

About 14,000 letters (private, not epistles) have been preserved from Greek and Roman antiquity. Their average length is 87 words, ranging in length from 18 to 209 words; these are brief by most standards. The letters of literary men like Cicero are not entirely suitable to Deissmann's classification; they were directed to persons and yet the authors wrote with a view to publication. Cicero averages 295 words, ranging from 22 words to 2,530 words. By these standards the New Testament letters are long. The 13 epistles which bear the name of Paul averaged 1,300 words, ranging from 7,101 (Romans) to 658 (Titus) and 335 (Philemon).

Deissmann judged that all the letters of Paul were letters, not epistles; that is, they were personal communications on matters of private interest with no view to general publication. That the readers may have shared them with others, with or without the bidding of Paul, does not change their purpose and definition. We often expect our letters to be shared, or invite our correspondents to share them; yet they remain personal private communications. In moral theology a letter is called a "natural" secret which cannot be invaded without sin. The person whose rights are protected in this moral principle is not the writer of the letter but the recipient; the recipient becomes the owner of the letter by the donation of the writer. The moral principle involved illustrates the problems of reading the letters of perfect strangers, which is what Paul and the church of Corinth are to modern readers. We know little about them except from the letters. An epistle is addressed to us; a letter is written from a naturally private situation. If the situation is not known, the letter is unintelligible unless the letter itself discloses enough of the situation. This problem will recur when we deal with the letters; the reader should not wonder that the letters are sometimes obscure. He should rather be pleasantly surprised that they are not more difficult than they are. We may call it exegesis, but the common name for reading other people's mail is snooping.

Deissmann classified the other New Testament letters (except II-III John) as epistles. An address to the twelve tribes of the Diaspora (James 1:1) or to the exiles of the Diaspora in Pontus, Galatia, Cappadocia, Asia and Bithynia cannot be realistic. The First Letter of John does not even have the letter form. Again the principle of the epistle permits us to approach these documents as addressed to us as much as to anyone else; one need not snoop into private affairs, to employ the figure used above, in order to read them with intelligence.

Like us, Greeks and Romans employed conventional forms of address and conclusion in letters. When compared with ours their forms were simple. The first sentence was "A to B, good health." The address by location was necessary but not in the letter; it was given to the messenger. Since there was no postal service, letters were given to someone who was traveling to the destination of the letter. The letter was concluded by a single Greek or Latin word—"good health"—(not the same word used in the introduction). This was the only word which was written by the correspondent, and it served in place of the signature, which was not used. As we point out below, the letter was dictated to a professional scribe.

One observes immediately that the New Testament letters do not follow these conventional forms; and the numerous letters preserved from ancient times assure us that this was a notable departure from convention. It is evident that these formulae would identify the writer as a fellow Christian; this need not have been the purpose of the formulae, but it seems that correspondence between Christians developed its own conventional formulae. The letters bearing the name of Paul all identify him by some Christian title. Instead of the wish for good health he opens with a blessing or a thanksgiving or a doxology, which in a few cases reaches notable dimensions, so as to become nearly a short Christian creed. In eight of the letters, others in addition to Paul are named with him as senders of the letters. The concluding formula is not a wish for good health but a blessing, most frequently a wish for "grace." Paul evidently had trouble, like many of us, in finding a place to end his letters. There are often greetings given by name both to people at the receiving end and from people at the sending end. There are hurried brief afterthoughts fired off without plan or order, like conversations which are terminated by the departure of a train. The Epistle to the Hebrews has no introductory formula, but it has the concluding formula.

Dictation, as mentioned, was the normal means of producing letters. Many of the ancient letters which have been preserved were letters of the poor, so dictation was not the luxury which it is in modern times. There is no way of knowing how common literacy was; perhaps the scribe had to be hired to read the letter as well as to write it. But literacy does not appear to have been the determining factor in dictation. Even people who could read and write did not think of submitting their readers to unprofessional penmanship. It was probably not even a concern for legibility, but rather a concern for beauty, or at least for neatness, which imposed dictation as a social canon. Most people availed themselves of professional public scribes. The rich and the official class and professional writers had scribes of their own; most of these were probably slaves, like Cicero's scribe Tiro. Paul had scribes in his Christian communities, and they surely formed a part of the company of associates with whom he traveled. Tertius has left his name in Romans 16:22. No generally used method of shorthand is attested for ancient times; if the scribe had his own way of abbreviating the dictation, it would have been like the personal abbreviations students use in taking lecture notes. These do not permit the exact recording of words spoken at the normal pace, the kind of record which the modern stenographer and stenotypist can produce.

The factor of dictation becomes of considerable importance and of some uncertainty in determining the part of the true "author," such as Paul, and the part of his amanuenses in the production of the epistles. Without shorthand the ancient writer could dictate words only at the pace at which the words could be written. Otherwise he would talk out what he wanted to say and leave the formation of sentences to the amanuensis; he could then edit what the scribe wrote. A skilled and experienced scribe, especially if he had done considerable work for a single man, could quite easily become familiar with the writer's style of speech, his characteristic words and phrases, and the general cast of his thought. He could produce a parody of what the writer might be expected to say on almost any subject. The author by his revision could make the document a quite faithful record of what he had said and of the way he said it. Still another way was to allow the scribe to compose the entire epistle; the modern secretary can be given a letter to answer and with knowledge both of the situation and of the writer can produce a letter which need not be altered.

One does not think of the poems of Horace or of the speeches of Cicero as being produced in the third way, or even in the second way; yet the ancient scribe certainly had more skill than we think he had. As for the letters of Paul, we are not sure. If there is such a thing as a personal literary style it was possessed by Paul. It is mostly this highly personal style, as we shall see, which enables modern critics to doubt his authorship of letters where it is missing. One need read very little of Paul's letters, especially if one selects some of the more highly emotional passages, to have serious doubts that these were produced by dictation word for word. The reader is invited to test himself and see whether he can sustain an emotionally charged speech if he is forced to utter it at the speed at which even a rapid writer can copy it. These are reasons for thinking that Paul generally—not necessarily always—simply talked, and that the scribe caught as much of the content, the mood and the language as he could. We observe again that it was his professional skill to write in the style of the speech of anyone who dictated to him. It is a professional skill, but it is not impossible; and Paul must have been a sharply defined personality with a sharply defined personal style of speech. The fact emerges that the letters of Paul are produced partly by Paul and partly by his scribes. Not all modern interpreters, perhaps not even most of them, would attribute this much of the composition to Paul's scribes; but it seems probable, and to this interpreter most probable, that Paul did not write his letters as this author, for example, writes these commentaries. These are all mine; I do not think the letters are all Paul's. This does not make Paul's scribes what we call ghostwriters, sometimes identified by name when illiterate athletes publish their memoirs "as told to X." The modern writer of an autobiography will not infrequently hire a professional writer because, while he is literate, he has no practice in writing. This relationship is more like the relationship of Paul to his scribes than the relationship of one who dictates to a stenographer. One can also liken the relationship of Paul with his scribes to the position of the modern executive or literary secretary, who is much more highly paid than a stenographer because of the proved skill not only in writing like the employer, but also frequently in thinking like him. The work of these unseen collaborators must be considered in the questions of Pauline authorship of the epistles; for in fact there is no epistle which is purely and entirely the work of Paul (Philemon is a possible exception).

A further possibility suggests itself. Besides scribes, Paul had helpers and collaborators in the ministry proper, and we know the names of many of them. Sosthenes, Timothy and Silvanus are mentioned with Paul as having sent epistles. Is it possible that some letters from Paul were produced like modern letters from popes and bishops, meaning that they come from the office and not from the person? Obviously Paul had nothing like the modern ecclesiastical curia, but neither was he a solitary man who handled all his own paper work. Against this as a general theory of the composition of the letters is the highly personal style already mentioned; in the ancient world as in the modern world, bureaucracies spoke a language of their own resembling the language of no living human being. Nevertheless, we are not committing an anachronism if we suppose that Paul might instruct Timothy and Tertius to produce a letter in his name.

Letters are occasional by definition. All letters are answers, either to a prior letter or to the spoken word or to a situation. What evokes the letter is known to the writer and to the recipient, and it need not be mentioned in the letter. The scope of the letter is determined by that to which it is a response. We know of no letter in the New Testament which was a response to a request for a complete exposition of the gospel or of Christian teaching. If a letter contains elements or fragments of the gospel or of Christian teaching, they are given in response to a question, explicit or implicit, which we have not heard and can only deduce. One sees the dangers latent in the assumption that the epistles contain a summary of doctrine. It would be sheer coincidence if all the epistles together added up to such a summary. They are documents of faith in a broad and vague sense. The four Gospels are also documents of faith; most of the contents of the four Gospels are not reflected in the epistles of Paul. His own "gospel," which he mentions several times (Romans 2:16; I Corinthians 15:1; Galatians 1:11, 2:2) is nowhere given in the epistles, and we cannot even conjecture how the gospel which he calls "mine" was in any sense his own, or why he should have thought it worth insisting upon. In the church, great stress is laid upon instruction in Christian doctrine, which begins in childhood with the catechism and ideally (in the Catholic church) is continued through adult life. If such a body of doctrine existed in the apostolic church we do not have it, and the importance of doctrinal instruction is reflected in few of the epistles, and those rather late. Students of the epistles feel compelled to construct a doctrinal synthesis upon them, but they must remember that what they desire is not found in the epistles. The reader should not feel disappointed that the epistles do not give him a complete catechism of apostolic doctrine; that complete catechism never existed. The apostolic church did not think that a doctrinal system was of primary importance; in fact, it left no evidence to suggest that it thought a doctrinal system was of any importance.

Where, then, does the emphasis fall in the epistles? Certainly the writers make efforts to correct what we could call doctrinal errors. Some of these are so remote from modern experience that they are meaningless to modern readers; but the corrections furnish occasion for the writers to state belief in a way in which it would not have been stated except in response to error. Paul's controversies about circumcision and the Law deal with problems which are dead in the modern church; his declarations of the centrality of Christ and of Christian freedom are never out of date, nor have they been completely apprehended by the church—at the time he wrote or subsequently. The emphasis in the epistles is not on doctrine, which is a matter of knowing, but on the Christian life, which is a matter of being and doing. The Christian *is* something; he is not a Christian by knowing something.

We do not mean that the interest of the epistles is moralistic. Just as a Christian does not become a Christian by learning a doctrinal system, so he does not become a Christian by meeting the demands of an ethical code. This question will meet us again often when we treat of Paul's attitude toward the Jewish Law. The rich young man in the Gospels (Mark 10:17-31; Matthew 19:16-30; Luke 18:18-30) asked Jesus what he should do to win eternal life and was told to keep the commandments—that is, to be an observant Jew. His question, whether there was a further possibility, led to demands which he could not meet. These further possibilities are of major interest to the writers of the epistles, especially to Paul. Jews at that time were convinced that morality of the Law was far above the morality of the Hellenistic-Roman world, as indeed it was. But there were philosophical schools which taught a substantially sound morality, of which the Stoics were the best examples. Neither Jews nor Stoics reached very many people. Had Christianity been merely a new ethical code, it would have had no revolutionary quality. Nor would it have had the universal appeal which it ultimately manifested in the Hellenistic-Roman world. The

Christian proclamation denied that there was any ceiling to the moral possibilities of man; it preached a morality which could not be incorporated into a code.

The epistles as occasional documents deal with questions about the practical fulfillment of the Christian life. The gospel was Palestinian in origin and in expression, and its preachers depended heavily on the Jewish scriptures for their language and their themes. When the Christian life was proclaimed to Gentiles, it appeared as something exotic, not only religiously but culturally. It is evident from the epistles that many Gentiles grasped the invitation to become Jews more easily than they grasped the invitation to become Christians. Jews observed the Law by settling in Jewish communities where everyone shared Jewish obligations and Jewish practices. It seems that Christians never formed Christian ghettos within which the practice of Christian morality would be easier because everyone in the neighborhood practiced it. The Christian moral imperative, unlike the Jewish Law, did not go into details; it remained a general mandate the execution of which was left to the initiative and the moral judgment of the individual. It is not surprising that particular questions arose; most Christians since have been afraid to trust their own initiative and moral judgment and have sought specific directions from their spiritual leaders.

The writers of the epistles refused to be specific as the Jewish rabbis and the modern moral theologians have been specific. It appears that the major industries of Corinth were shipping and prostitution; yet Paul's letters to Corinth are not as specific as we expect them to be, or as they would be if we ourselves wrote them. There is still no ceiling on the moral possibilities of the Christian life, even at Corinth. Paul did not face explicitly the philosophical and sociological statement that people can reach that moral level which their society allows them to reach. Had he to reject this explicitly as a moral principle, he would have rejected it. As a simple statement of fact and not a moral principle he was as well aware of it as we are. It perhaps comes to this: there was no prefabricated Christian model which Paul imported to Corinth and taught the Corinthians to operate. A genuine living Christianity was not produced in Corinth by the preaching of the gospel, still less by instruction in Christian doctrine and Christian ethics. Genuine living Christianity appeared in Corinth only when genuine living Christians appeared, who alone would decide what was required to be a genuine living Christian in Corinth. In this enterprise Paul could help by encouragement and by answering some questions; he could neither do it or show them how to do it. Paul spent eighteen months in Corinth, it seems, and never returned to the city. This does not leave time for specific and detailed instructions, nor does it indicate that Paul had any intention of giving such instructions, either in his teaching or in his letters.

In the treatment of most of the epistles the question of authorship will arise. Probably many readers will quickly become impatient with these discussions, some because the question is raised at all, others because they feel that to question the authorship is in some way to question the sacredness of the book, and still others because they see no profit in such discussions. Gregory the Great in the preface to his commentary on Job said that it is a waste of time to look for the author of Job (who is unknown) since the Holy Spirit wrote the book. Certainly Gregory spoke for many of the faithful when he said this. He did not speak for modern students of the Bible, however, who must reverently depart from the mind of the holy doctor in this respect. When the Holy Spirit wrote through Matthew and Mark, he did not write in the style of Luke and John. The only way in which the interpreter can grasp the mind of the Holy Spirit in these writings is to investigate the minds of the men who produced the writings. Since the Holy Spirit does not speak the same way through different men, the study of these men becomes of primary importance.

That there is a general human tendency to attribute literature to famous figures is not questioned. However, the simple application of this principle does not explain all the critical problems of the Bible. Why should an epistle be attributed to Jude, surely mentioned only three times outside of the epistle? Why should Gospels be attributed to two obscure disciples and one of the more obscure apostles? One is tempted to say that these works could be attributed to these men for no other reason than that they wrote them; yet neither is this a sure principle. In the second century "apostolic" writings were held in special veneration in the church, and this was a preliminary step in their establishment as Scripture; we do not know that this veneration was extended to apostolic writings in the apostolic generation. When were the "apostolic" writings collected? For what purpose were they collected? How were they recognized as "apostolic"? These are questions to which we have no answers.

It is often disconcerting to those who begin the study of the Bible to learn that the simple attribution of a work to a name is not generally to be accepted without examination. Why, they wonder, must critics make trouble for the simple faithful by raising these doubts? The basis of criticism is in the text itself. I have mentioned the highly personal style of Paul. As one reads the epistles this personal style comes through, even in translation. To go from one extreme to another, one cannot fail to notice a different tone in the pastoral epistles from the tone in Galatians and I-II Corinthians. We have already noticed that the work of the amanuenses allows room for some variations in style. The question is how much variation can be allowed. One moves from differences of style to differences of thought, which is an even more subtle area. We are not dealing with differences as obvious, for example, as those between the campaign speeches of opposing presidential candidates, nor with less obvious disputes and hidden contradictions. The epistles are all concerned with the same subject matter, the Christian gospel and its explanation. They do not even reflect the difference between Paul and the Judaizers with whom he contends; no New Testament document reflects the Christian Judaism which Paul describes. How then does the critic pretend to find differences of thought which are so clearly marked that they demand different persons? Critics readily admit that the kind of evidence which ends discussion is never available. It is rather the careful assembling of points of detail, each of itself unimportant, into a pattern which is explained with great difficulty as the work of a single mind. It is abstractly possible that I might be the ghostwriter of the pastoral letters of Cardinal Carberry. The texts make it highly improbable, but I do not know whether a convincing argument could be mounted on the comparison of the texts alone.

What is meant by differences of thought will become clear, it is hoped, in the treatment of the separate epistles; our concern here is merely to establish the validity of the principle, and probably most readers will admit its validity once it is explained. They may still wonder about the validity of critical methods for determining decisive differences of thought. The use of such methods demands a much closer analysis of documents than the reader is accustomed to give. What does the church mean, for example, to its modern members? We have heard much in the last ten years about the church as the mystical body of Christ, as the pilgrim people of God, and as a juridical entity. These views are certainly different; they are not so opposed to each other that those who hold them cannot remain with the one church. They are in sufficient opposition to give us reason to suppose that no document bearing the signature of Paul VI will designate the juridical understanding of the church as archaic and meaningless for the modern Catholic. It is true that a close analysis of the documents is not required to perceive this difference; yet in most of the documents in which this difference appears there is a conscious effort to minimize it. We recognize the difference because we are contemporaries of the discussion. We are not contemporaries to the differences which we think we see in the epistles. A close examination which goes beyond style is illustrated by the word count, on which critics place some stress. All of us who write have a definite vocabulary which we ourselves have not analyzed. When an examination of Paul shows that certain characteristic words do not occur over a stretch of perhaps several pages, or that another stretch shows words which occur nowhere else in Paul, we are not convinced that we are dealing with different authors; as one who writes, I think that an inquiry into the variation of vocabulary is altogether reasonable. The appearance of certain words on a page could make me wonder whether I wrote it; and I can always detect sentences which an editor has recast—in his unenlightened judgment, for the better. It is possible that such a strange word introduced into my writing or the recasting of a sentence may give the thought a direction which I did not intend it to take. To question the validity of the method is legitimate in each instance, for the method may be applied in texts where the material is not present; but the reader can be assured that those who write themselves are quite satisfied that the method is generally valid, and is more often right than wrong.

Here we must recall the way in which the letters were composed, and the part of the amanuenses in their composition. We have adverted to the way in which a skillful secretary can reproduce the style of the principal writer; not all secretaries have this skill to an equal degree, and one can think of instances in which it would not be necessary to invoke this skill. We simply do not know how many amanuenses Paul employed. His highly personal style emerges with an even quality in the letters which are accepted without question as Paul's. In the other letters it does not emerge as clearly and in some letters critics believe it does not emerge at all. Can this difference be explained through the possibility that Paul dictated these letters at a normal pace instead of word for word, a pace which was too rapid for the amanuensis who, lacking the skill of Paul's other secretaries, was unable to catch his style and tone? Hardly any critic now believes that this explains the composition of the doubtful letters; and they might be more sympathetic were it not for the hard core of seven letters which in style of language and patterns of thought clearly belong together. In a few of the other letters there is a possibility that they were not composed by Paul but simply commissioned by him.

For the other letters the same critical methods are not applicable because there is not enough material for comparison. Critics are sure that the two epistles of Peter were written by different persons; if the canons of literary criticism have any value, they are valid here. Two of the three letters of John are so brief that they afford little comparative material. James and I Peter could be the work of James and Peter as well as of anyone else; we know so little about both men that we can neither affirm nor deny the traditional attribution. Jude is unknown except for the epistle. Hebrews is anonymous; the attribution to Paul is not early, and the style of Hebrews is even further from the seven letters of Paul than the doubtful letters. Strictly speaking, the critical question cannot be raised outside of the Pauline letters. Stylistically, I John belongs with the Gospel of John; neither document belongs with Revelation. Whether John the Apostle wrote any of the documents is neither proved nor denied by these stylistic relations; it is clear that John the Apostle cannot be responsible for all of the documents bearing the name of John.

If reasons appear why the epistles should not be attributed to the men whose names they traditionally bear, one may ask how they came to have the traditional attribution. No certain answer can be given to this, for we have no history of the New Testament books in the church for the first few centuries. It is evident that the epistles were first found in scattered places, and one assumes that the first owners of the documents knew where they came from. This assumption is subject to certain reservations, to be explained shortly. We should like to know who first thought of gathering them all into a single collection, but before this happened there must have been collections of the epistles of Paul. Modern scholars have pointed out that in the ancient world there were letter-books, the work of scribes who produced the letters and kept copies. It has been suggested that these letter-books may explain what appear to be certain dislocations in the letters of Paul. Such a letter-book would have been the earliest collection of the letters of Paul, and it would have been made not for religious reasons but for practical reasons, if one may distinguish the two in this way. Paul and his amanuenses wanted a record of what he had written to his correspondents, and there was no thought of collecting the inspired words of God or of the holy man. The copy of Galatians, we think, was used in the preparation of Romans. That such a letter-book existed does not impose the conclusion that the New Testament collection came from such a letter-book. In any case, we have to suppose that the first owner of the letter-book knew who produced the letters.

How did false attributions arise? We prefer to think that they arose from simple error rather than from deliberate deception. If Paul produced letters as an office rather than as a person, then the attribution was not simply false. The Roman Pontiff's writings reach a thousand printed pages a year; they would still be attributed to him if he did not write a single line, and even if he did not revise and edit them. "The Holy See" signifies an office, also known as Paul VI, and everyone recognizes this. It is perhaps more accurate to suppose that some of the letters may have been produced by the office rather than by "the Pauline school," as some writers have called it. We have noticed that the office (or school) included as many as a dozen names: Apollos, Aquila and Priscilla, Barnabas, Timothy, Tertius, Sosthenes, Titus, Epaphroditus, Tychicus, Aristarchus, Mark, Luke, Silvanus. These are clearly Paul's helpers mentioned in the epistles. They need not all have been in his entourage at once —indeed the names mentioned certainly were not—but they are numerous enough and literate enough to have produced documents in the name of Paul and by his authority, perhaps a very general authority. They could have remained a group even after the death of Paul, and they were more likely to have been interested in collecting his letters than anyone else. Could they have produced letters from the collective personality called "Paul" even after he died? If the critics are right about the doubtful epistles, this must have happened.

We often attribute to the early Christians a naivete which we think we do not have. We think that if someone found or brought a document which was presented as a letter of Paul or Peter or John, there was no one present to ask whether this document could be authenticated. There may not have been, or he may have won no attention; but the early Christians were probably no more naive than we are, who think that the name of Paul at the top of the printed page settles the question. The tendency to attribute literature or art to illustrious names is not limited to early Christians, and the number of people who are equipped to make a critical examination of literature or art has never been larger. At the same time, we must remember that the early Christians attributed some New Testament books to some very obscure people. The desire to have a book written by a famous man does not solve the problem of false attribution.

This leads us to the problem of pseudonymity, the conscious and deliberate attachment of a name to the document of someone who is not the author. As a literary device this is known in modern literature; we think nothing of it because it is intended to deceive no one and does not. If a very simple and uninformed reader should be deceived by this attribution, the author would say that he never expected such a person to read his work; he might even say that he never suspected a person so simple existed. Most critics doubt that pseudonymous works in the ancient world can all be explained in this way. A great number of such works were produced in Judaism, some of which found their way into the Greek Old Testament; others are preserved in the Pseudepigrapha. We doubt that writers who wrote under the name of Enoch or Ezra seriously thought that anyone would take these works as written by the men whose names they bear, or that readers did so take the works seriously; we simply do not know. The books of Enoch are quoted in Jude 14-15; the author seems to take the authorship of Enoch seriously. The claim of antiquity, if it were believed, would lend the book an authority it did not have. In our ethics this would be dishonest if it were a serious purpose; and I do not see anything in the ethics of the ancient world which would make it less dishonest then. Most Bible readers shudder at the thought of accepting as the word of God the writings of a dishonest author. That he may have posed under an alien name for a noble purpose does not make his action honest.

Generally, II Timothy is regarded as post-Pauline. We may assume that it was produced by the Pauline group mentioned above. We may suppose that this group thought it carried on the teaching and the authority of Paul with respect to the churches he founded. We are very nearly compelled to suppose that this letter was not addressed to Timothy, who could not be addressed in these terms by anyone else but Paul. We can suppose that those who received this letter (more probably, this epistle) knew in what sense it was Pauline. Under what pretext did a letter known by its writers and its readers not to be a personal communication of Paul contain such intensely personal lines as those with which the letter concludes? Did these serve any purpose except to make the mask more convincing? Were they taken from an earlier letter of Paul and added to a post-Pauline composition? This is scarcely less dishonest than the fiction of personal Pauline authorship. Yet this is perhaps the easiest solution to the problem, to suppose that an original letter of Paul was edited and re-edited until it finally reflected Paul's personal situation more accurately than it reflected the conditions of the churches during Paul's life. This example shows the pains which the interpreter must take if he is not to adopt the obvious solution and say that the authors of the post-Pauline letters were liars, but that there was something in the ethical environment which kept them and their readers from thinking so.

It must, however, be accepted that the authors of pseudonymous works were honestly convinced that they were authentic spokesmen of the men whose names they used. If we are correct in supposing the continued existence of a Pauline group after the death of Paul, it is easy to understand their attitude. In the first generations of the church there were no spokesmen of "the church," as the bishops and the Pope became in subsequent centuries. We would understand their minds better if we knew more about the divisions at Corinth, in which the parties identified themselves with Paul, Apollos, Cephas—and Christ, as though he were another apostle; obviously they meant more. Paul called himself usually an apostle of Jesus Christ. His group could not make this claim, but they could be the spokesmen of the apostle of Jesus Christ. There was no pontifical or episcopal authority which could sit in judgment on them as superior. I recognize that the implications of this view for church structure are more than trivial; but the unity of the church in the apostolic age was hardly reflected at all in its organization. I am supposing that the Pauline group was on its way to developing into a hierarchical organization; that it possessed the Pauline documents; that it regarded itself as the custodian and the sole authentic interpreter of Paul's "gospel"; that it felt itself empowered to speak and to write to the Pauline churches in the name and the authority of Paul. I say on the way to becoming a hierarchical authority; it is evident that when Paul established a church he established it as independent and self-propelled, and dealt with it no further except on the basis of friendship or of consultation. To him the apostolate was a commission to preach the gospel where it had not been preached, not to be a superbishop of the churches he had founded. One does not think that his most intimate associates would have been the first to betray his own ideas of the apostolate and the local church.

So far one must theorize, it seems, in order to deal with a few documents which are pseudonymous. The theory is perhaps more elaborate than necessary and far from surely founded in the history of the apostolic church. But the history of the apostolic church is extremely scanty; and these considerations seem to suit what is known of the apostolic church and to suggest some insights into what is not known about that church. We should point out that the book of Acts is not a complete history of the apostolic church, nor even of the churches of Paul. The epistles of Paul are related to the life of Paul only by conjecture and with great difficulty. They are related to the book of Acts with even more difficulty. It may surprise some readers as well as disappoint them that a close study of the epistles, and I mean those which are unquestionably the work of Paul, leads one to serious problems in the book of Acts, and the closer the study the more serious the problems become. What seems to be a straightforward narrative in Acts ceases to be straightforward when we compare it with Paul's account of his life, meager as that account is. Nowhere does Paul mention the council of Jerusalem (Acts 15). Of all the reasons alleged for his not mentioning it (and its omission is something like the omission of the battle of Waterloo in the letters of the Duke of Wellington) the most probable reason is that he never heard of it, for the good reason that as Luke described it the council never happened. Interpreters are compelled to conclude that Luke summarized in a single event a chain of events which was more complex and protracted. The modern writer does not compose history in this manner, but it should make him careful in using Luke uncritically as a source. In fact Luke does not mention the fact that Paul wrote any letters. He does not mention the problems of Corinth, although it is impossible to suppose that he was at all close to Paul and unaware of them. The problem of Judaism, which we shall see is large in the epistles of Paul, is not mentioned by Luke except in his account of the discussion at Jerusalem. One would not deduce from his account the passion with which Paul spoke of the question of Judaism. Interpreters generally conclude that Luke wished to bury decently a bitter controversy which was no longer active. One appreciates this delicacy, but it is not helpful to a historian who wishes to study the quarrels.

The reader may notice that in the course of this exposition we always prefer the epistles if they seem to be in opposition to the book of Acts. In some instances one must make a clear choice, and it seems not only honest but necessary to explain the basis of our procedure. Luke did not intend to write the kind of history the modern interpreter thinks he needs in order to interpret the epistles. It seems altogether probable that it never occurred to Luke that anyone might want to interpret the epistles. He may have thought that someone might wonder how the apostolic church could really be called Christian and thought he should write an answer to that question. If this was his purpose, he was the first to deal with a problem which every church historian has had to meet.

The order in which the epistles will be read in this program is not the order in which they appear in the New Testament. This arrangement is not made purely for the purpose of confusing the reader. The epistles of Paul are arranged in the New Testament in an order which has neither logic nor history to recommend it. First are the letters to the churches, then the letters to persons. Within these two groups the letters are arranged in the order of size; they go from the longest, Romans, to the shortest, Philemon. I think the readers will agree that nothing will be gained by reading the letters in this order. Hebrews, as we have remarked, was not at first considered an epistle of Paul, and it stands outside the order.

The other seven epistles are traditionally called the "Catholic" epistles, often rendered in English versions as they were designated in the Authorized Version, the "General" epistles. These letters have no particular designation like the letters of Paul, and were considered as addressed to the whole church. We have noticed that they are epistles rather than letters, and that some of the addresses are unreal. These we can read in the order in which they appear in the New Testament; if we could ascertain their relative dates, they could be read in this order, but nothing would be gained; they are independent compositions.

The genuinely Pauline letters are the oldest writings of the New Testament, older than the Gospels and Acts. The reader is naturally inclined to presuppose the Gospels when he reads the epistles. This is a serious misunderstanding. Paul never refers to the events narrated in the Gospels except the death and resurrection of Jesus, and his allusions to these events are so meager in detail that we cannot reconstruct the version in which his congregations heard of the passion and resurrection. No words of Jesus in the Gospel are quoted, and no miracles are mentioned. The sole point of reference is the institution of the Eucharist; Paul gives one of the four versions of this (Matthew, Mark, Luke) and the four are remarkably close to each other. It is thought that the source of all four was a liturgical formula. We have noticed that the epistles are occasional documents intended to respond to situations, and it is illegitimate to conclude that the words and actions of Jesus, the materials of the Gospels, were mentioned as little in Paul's preaching (his "gospel") as they are in the letters. Yet this conclusion seems to be recommended. It suggests that not only are the letters of Paul prior to the Gospels, they are prior to any narratives which might have resembled the Gospels. It is difficult to imagine Paul's not using such material if he had it. And we cannot help wondering how many other apostles had such material available.

We have already mentioned that it is difficult to locate the epistles in the life of Paul, mainly because we do not know the life of Paul well. For example, four epistles (Philippians, Philemon, Colossians, Ephesians) are traditionally called the "Epistles of the Captivity" because they contain references to imprisonment (Phil. 1:7, 13, 14; Phm. 1, 9, 10, 23; Eph. 3:1, 4:1, 6:20; Col. 4:3, 18). The only imprisonment mentioned in Acts was the long detention in Caesarea and in Rome with which the book ends. Philippians can hardly be placed in this period; Philemon can be, but Ephesians and Colossians must be included in the doubtful letters. One is tempted to say that it is not important to relate the epistles to the life of Paul, but we say it is unimportant simply because we cannot do it.

We have adverted to the absence of a doctrinal system not only in Paul, but in the apostolic church as a whole. In reading the epistles in the probable order of composition we are not attempting to show the development of a system. In fact the letters reveal more about Paul the man than about any alleged Pauline system. And the life and character of an authentic Christian are certainly as worthy of study, even of prayerful meditation, as a doctrinal system. Paul's concern was the formation of Christians, not of doctrine; and in forming Christians he could not help revealing his own conversion. The result is not a spiritual autobiography of the type which has often been produced in the modern world; but it is a confession of the meaning of Christ to Paul as a person. This meaning is what Paul attempts to communicate as well as the proclamation of the gospel and the "teaching." This is the principal element in the personal style of the epistles which we have had occasion to mention several times, the depth of Paul's personal commitment to Christ, what he calls faith. It is one of the reasons why scholars doubt the personal authorship of Paul in letters which are comparatively cool in tone; it does not seem that a man whose commitment was so impassioned could ever speak of it coolly.

The personal tone also comes from Paul's relations to the churches. The letters are as far as they could be from the impersonal tone (often descending to bureaucratic jargon) of communications from modern pontifical and diocesan offices. These modern communications are written from strangers to strangers; there is nothing one can do immediately about this. No reader finds anything feigned in the family tone of Galatians and I-II Corinthians. Paul embarrasses the modern churchman because he has a personal commitment to the members of his churches as strong as his personal commitment to Christ, for he identifies the members with Christ. Regretfully the modern churchman must often recognize that he has not achieved this identification nor this commitment. Neither can he sincerely show the feeling which Paul shows because he does not feel that deeply.

There are some interesting points of development, however, and these will appear in the exposition of the various epistles. The reader will notice in the early letters a candid and unquestioned expectation of the Second Coming; in fact, this expectation was the occasion of the Thessalonian letters. As one proceeds through the letters there is no explicit modification of this expectation; it simply ceases to appear. By the time of the pastoral epistles, which modern critics deny to Paul, the writer has reached almost the modern attitude toward the Second Coming; I would say this means that we believe in it, but that we simply do not make it a factor in our faith or our doctrine. It is so remote as to be meaningless.

The question of the relation of Christian faith to the Jewish Law is the main issue in Galatians and part of the main issue in Romans. This indeed is an illustration of development.

Paul, it seems, took a position in which he had almost no support outside of his own group. I have long thought that his reticence in naming his opponents signifies that these opponents were important people. The two letters show how deeply Paul had to go into the meaning of the saving act of God in Christ in order to justify his own affirmation of freedom from the Law. What was an immediate response in Galatians becomes much more reflective in Romans. Romans is often called the nearest thing to a Pauline synthesis of doctrine; but the doctrinal construction was elicited by the simple question of whether or not a Christian was obliged to observe the Jewish Law.

In the study of any author students are directed to his intellectual and cultural background. When we consider the critical questions we have already mentioned, we must confess that this will often be the background of some Christian of the first century. This can be illuminating; this background is so different from ours that we can never study it enough. Yet even for Paul, the best known of the New Testament writers, and hardly typical of the rest, what do we know? He was a Jew; most Christians of the first generation were. He was a rabbi; we are not sure of any other New Testament writer who was, but they were not uncommon in the apostolic church. We do not know, and this is annoying, who were his Christian teachers and what they taught him. He once insisted that he had not learned his gospel from men but from a revelation of Jesus Christ (Gal. 1:11-12). All of the original disciples could make this claim. Yet there was a common belief which was becoming a common tradition; we cannot believe that Paul formed his proclamation entirely free of the influence of others, and the phrase does not imply so much. Whether the background of Paul's Christian doctrine was extensive or not, he has left us no information about it. In Acts 22:3 Luke quotes Paul as naming his rabbinical teacher, Gamaliel; but neither Luke nor Paul names a Christian teacher. We cannot know Paul better by a study of his background unless we study the content and method of rabbinical teaching of the first century. But while Paul can and does occasionally talk and argue as a rabbi, he is not a rabbi; he is something new and original which cannot be explained as simply a product of his background. He was also a product of Roman-Hellenistic civilization; and for what it is worth he is one of the most urban of writers, ancient or modern. Where the Gospels are full of allusions to the Palestinian countryside, Paul shows no more awareness of the countryside than the resident of Manhattan. As the apostle of the *goyim* (Gentiles) he was acquainted with them and their world. The student of Paul must also acquaint himself with that world, the world of Antioch, Ephesus, Corinth and Rome.

Jesus himself was a Palestinian villager, and this meant that he was at home in a small community of peasants and craftsmen. The interpretation of the Palestinian village Messiah in the Roman-Hellenistic cities was committed to a man whose home was those cities. This was the first and the most important leap which the gospel made from one culture to another. The interpretation of Paul was so important that there has never been a lack of critics to say that Christianity is more Pauline than Christian. On the other hand, the adversaries of Paul believed that the Gentile must become a Jew in order to become a Christian. The letters of Paul are the first Christian rejection of this attempt to identify Christianity with a culture or a nation, and to affirm that the scope of the saving act of God in Christ is as wide as humanity itself; and the principle is not invalidated because humanity is much wider than Paul knew. He rejected any racial or national or cultural predisposition for faith. Christians must admit that they have still not embraced this Pauline interpretation. Tribalism is more native to man than cosmopolitanism. Paul was not the first cosmopolitan; the word and the idea were invented by Stoic philosophers. To present Christianity as a genuine world faith it was necessary that there should be a man who was, as he emphatically affirmed, an authentic Jew and who was at home in the great world cities of his time.

Important as the background of Paul is, we can do little but study rabbinic Judaism and Roman-Hellenistic culture; we know the mind and feelings of Paul better than we know his personal background. But we are dealing with letters which are responses to words and actions. We should like to know the churches of Paul and their situations. The church which we know best is, of course, the church of Corinth; it was the domestic problems of this church which elicited two of the four "great" letters. As we shall see, the nature of these problems must be ascertained mostly by conjecture. Not all of the churches to which Paul wrote were located in large and celebrated cities. Colossae, for instance, appears in the time of Paul to have been a depressed textile manufacturing city. Perhaps the inhabitants of Lowell, Mass. and Nashua, N.H., have a better insight into the epistle to the Colossians than other readers, but they have not displayed it. Lowell and Nashua are not confused by Gnostic speculations, which was the problem of the Colossians. To the extent to which it is possible, students of the New Testament search ancient records for information concerning the cities in which the churches were located; it is on such investigations that we base an earlier remark that the major industries of Corinth were shipping and prostitution. On the other hand, Paul wrote to Rome without any personal experience of the city or its church; and the epistle requires no more knowledge of Rome than Paul had. This is probably more than the average New Testament reader has. Yet do such studies tell us any more about the people of Paul's churches than a modern guide book tells us about New York or Chicago? The average resident of large cities is rather amused by popular guides and descriptions of his city prepared by nonresidents; he wonders how anyone in a brief visit to his city could have acquired so much misinformation so quickly.

Paul said of the Corinthians that there were not among them many wise, powerful and noble (I Cor. 1:26); this was probably true of all the churches of the epistles, for there are many indications that the church of the first century was a movement in the lower classes—the poor, casual laborers, and slaves. Such movements, then and now, generally do not attract the attention of the wise, the powerful and the noble. Infrequently such movements deserve more attention, for they develop into revolutions; but most such movements simply disappear in the course of time and are of interest only to historians and sociologists. Representatives of such movements are rarely articulate according to the standards of those who cultivate literature and the arts; and the speeches and occasional writings they produce are not of the quality which the educated demand. There is hardly any reason to suppose a higher degree of literacy in the Pauline churches than we should expect to find in modern churches in the inner city; and one is compelled to wonder whether the letters of Paul, read in his churches, were much better understood than they are when they are read in the modern liturgy. Paul wrote good, vigorous, popular Greek, not on the level of polite letters; but at times he is carried away by his subject and seems to forget his audience. One has visions of the congregation asking what he means; but who was to explain it?

We cannot think of a church without at least one specially trained person in charge. We count on him to manage the property and the doctrine. In a large parish there will be more than one trained person, and they will be assisted by a staff. We simply do not know what the structure of government and administration was in the churches of Paul. We are accustomed also to a uniform pattern of church government. If we move to a different city or even to a different country, we will seek the pastor of the parish in which we have happened to take up residence, secure that there will be a man who has this responsibility and that his functions will be much the same as those of the same officer in the place we left. Wherever we live we will find ourselves in a diocese which will be governed by a bishop. He will do the same things which we have always associated with bishops. There may have been a uniform structure in the apostolic churches. It is not reflected in the New Testament. In particular we find no officers which resemble bishops of dioceses and pastors of parishes. Paul wrote to the church or the saints at X. To whom was the letter delivered? Who opened it and read it to the congregation? Our ignorance of these matters shows how little we know of the organization of the churches of Paul. But is it necessary to know this? Paul does not mention organization possibly because he did not think it important, or less important than other things which he does mention—love, for instance. We find no letters of Paul in which someone is instructed to tell someone else what to do. Each letter seems addressed to each individual member of the church; and to each one is committed the execution of what is to be done. As we shall have occasion to point out, Paul thought that simple membership in the church was a charismatic office with responsibilities which one was empowered to fulfill by the gift of the Spirit. The Spirit was not a privilege of the ruling class; and in the churches of Paul no ruling class appears.

This does not imply that the Pauline churches were disorganized. We have lists of officers in the epistles to which we shall refer. It is most probable that the local church was "governed," insofar as it was necessary, by a committee. These were "overseers"; they were assisted by "helpers." We use these words in quotation marks rather than the English words which are developed from the Greek words, bishop and deacon; these officers as they later developed do not appear in the Pauline churches. When Paul founded a church he may have appointed these officers; after the foundation they were elected by the members of the congregation. The qualifications for the office, as far as we know, were moral; there were certainly no standards of professional knowledge and expertise. We return to the idea of charisma; if a church office was committed to a person, this was an expression of the decision of the Spirit and of the conferring of the gifts of the Spirit which enabled the person to fulfill the duties of the office.

The infrequent and obscure mention of church offices does lead one to conclude that the principal function of the church officers was almsgiving. If we are correct in identifying the social class of church members, then the entire congregation was drawn from the poor. Before any of the Gospels were written, the churches believed and taught that one who does not share what he has with the one who has not clings to more wealth than he needs. In a community of the poor it was understood that the members would see that no one was destitute. One would think that if this could be proclaimed to the poor, to whom sharing was itself an approach to destitution, it could more easily be proclaimed to those who are conscious of no material need. Neither in the early church nor the later church has it worked out quite that way.

There is a distinctive feature of the apostolic church which perhaps has not been noticed often enough by interpreters. The Greek word *hiereus,* priest, is not applied to any church officer in the New Testament. Both Judaism and pagan religions had sacred personnel, of which the priests were of the highest rank. The author of I Peter calls the whole church a royal priesthood, a holy nation (I Pt. 2:9). Judaism had its temple of Jerusalem, the one place in the world which God had chosen for sacrificial worship. Greek and Roman religions had great temples like the Parthenon, and the remains of these temples attest to the wealth that was spent in the proper decoration of the sacred place. The apostolic church had no holy place. The community assembled for worship in a house or a rented hall; they could not have been numerous. Each Christian represented the holy place where God dwelt; the body is the temple of the indwelling Holy Spirit (I Cor. 6:19). And there is no mention of sacred vestments or sacred vessels and apparatus. The more recent church has gone back to paganism and Judaism for the restoration of these symbols of the sacred.

There is here something more profound than the mere rejection of pomp, worthwhile as this rejection may be. It is the sacred itself, in the traditional sense of the term, which is rejected, the sacred personnel and place and apparatus which are as old as religion itself. The apostolic church instituted a revolution which, as remarked, has not been sufficiently noticed. Shall we say that the church made itself profane or that it made the whole world sacred? The alternatives are not that rigorous. Much of the contemporary discussion about the secular understands the sacred in the sense in which it was understood in Judaism and paganism, the sense which the

New Testament rejected. Those who share this rejection are only returning to the earliest church.

The radical sacred for Paul in the text quoted above is the human person. There and there alone God dwells. If he does not dwell in every man it is because he is denied admission to his own temple. God is experienced not in the pomp and symbolism of temple ritual but in the love which man, led by the Spirit, is capable of extending to his neighbor. There is no sacred place which is specialized for this act of cult nor is there a special class of persons upon whom this duty of cult lies. The symbolism of the sacred has often meant not only that one recognizes where God is to be found and who are his representatives but also where he is not and who are not his representatives. It permits man to act in the area of the secular as if God did not exist. To what extent the retention of pagan symbols of the sacred by the church has supported the atheism of the secular is too large a topic for discussion in this exposition. It would be a serious omission in the study of the New Testament not to mention it at all.

Chapter Two

EPISTLES TO THE THESSALONIANS

Thessalonica, the modern Saloniki in Greece, lay on the Via Egnatia, the Roman road which connected Italy with Byzantium. It had a good harbor, good roads and was the port of a prosperous countryside; the modern Saloniki is the second largest city of Greece. The epistles fit the narrative of the evangelization of Thessalonica in Acts 17:1-9, except that the condition of the church and the relations of Paul with its members seem to demand a longer stay than Acts suggests. The hostility of the Jews at Thessalonica (Acts 17:5-9, 13) is supported by I Th 2:14-16. This passage and the idolatry (I Th 1:9) from which the Thessalonians were converted suggest that the church of Thessalonica was largely Gentile.

There is no serious question among modern interpreters that I Th is a letter of Paul and that it is the earliest of the letters. It is generally placed about 50-51 A.D. The Pauline authorship of II Th has some difficulties. If II Th is, as it appears to be, a correction of a misunderstanding about the Second Coming which was occasioned by I Th, it is difficult to explain how it could have been written so close to I Th; for in the hypothesis that II Th is from Paul it must have been written a few weeks after I Th. Some interpreters have thought the correction goes so far as to contradict what is said in I Th. To most interpreters this is not clear. We have already adverted to a development in Paul's thought on the Second Coming: those who doubt that II Th is from Paul think the development has advanced so far that it demands a different writer. On the other hand, the literary style of II Th raises no questions whatever. One writer has observed that there are difficulties both in taking II Th as the work of Paul and in denying that it is his work; there are fewer difficulties in accepting it.

The open occasion of the letter was Paul's concern for the welfare of the new church. They were experiencing persecution; this was not the persecution of public authority, carried on through police and the courts, but a kind of neighborhood harassment which was probably something like the harassment minority groups often suffer in our contemporary cities. Paul leaves no doubt as to the persecutors; they are Jews, his own people, and he compares their actions in Thessalonica to their harassment of Christians in Palestine. According to his own testimony (Gal 1:13) and the narrative of Acts, Paul himself had played a large part in this harassment, which led to the death of Stephen (Acts 7), described as a lynching rather than a legal process; there is nothing to indicate that things in Thessalonica had gone so far. The Jews enjoyed certain privileges in Roman law conceded to their religious scruples. It appears that the Roman authorities did not at first distinguish the new sect from Jews, and the Jews wished to make it clear that they did not want the Christians to share the Jewish legal umbrella. The harassment which Paul implies goes beyond this; Jews regarded faith in Jesus Messiah as radical treason to Judaism, and this before Paul had developed his thesis on the Law (see Galatians and Romans). Many Christians, if not most at this early period, were Jewish Christians.

In order to reassure himself about Thessalonica Paul had sent Timothy to visit, being prevented from coming in person for reasons which he does not give. Timothy had probably reported other things to which Paul responds in the letter; these are not the open occasion of the letter, but whether his intention in treating these matters was as casual as he makes it appear is doubtful. The first response is to certain slanders laid against Paul by persons he does not mention; in fact he does not even expressly mention that they are charges. But a reasonably full exposition of his actions and his motives (2:1-12), and his denial that he was deluded, immoral, deceptive, fawning, covetous, vain or authoritarian is a remarkably full catalogue of denials, too full to be anything but a response to charges. Paul does not dignify them by calling them charges nor does he mention his accusers. They were probably the same Jews whom he calls persecutors. We meet similar defenses of the apostolate in Galatians and II Corinthians, but the adversaries are Judaizing Christians. These, it seems, had not yet appeared as Paul's adversaries.

Timothy had also reported some "shortcomings" in their faith (3:10). Of course the first was certainly sexual morality (4:1-8). In spite of what the modern reader may think, Christian sexual morality was more revolutionary in the Hellenistic-Roman cities than it is today. Externally at least, European society and culture have accepted the standards of Christian sexual morality for centuries, and those who openly reject them are forced to do it with a certain ferocious self-assertion. The resident of cities like Thessalonica thought no more of dropping in at the neighborhood brothel than he did of dropping in at a neighborhood bar; in fact they were normally the same installation. Sex was regarded as a normal psychophysical experience of pleasure like eating, drinking, sport, poetry and the theater. We could wish that Paul had left us some account of how he first told prospective converts that we must not live this way. It would be a technique we could still find useful. Christian morality here did not differ notably from Jewish morality; but Jewish morality was not proposed as a part of a world religion. Yet Paul refers only to "the life that you were meant to live: the life that God wants, as you learned from us" (4:1) and "the instructions we gave you on the authority of the Lord Jesus" (4:2). About a topic on which modern preachers have given entire series, Paul, in a more difficult situation, wrote eight verses.

Since Paul says that there is no need to write them about love of the brothers, we naturally wonder what their shortcoming was in this respect. Very probably we have to add 5:12-16 to these verses, where Paul seems to have decided to be more explicit. Christian love is a more subtle attitude than most Christians appreciate. Living quietly, attending to your own business and earning your sustenance seems less than heroic. Possibly we should also invoke II Th 3:10 in explanation; it may have been the imminent expectation of the end which led some believers to give up all interest in the daily obligations and urge the whole community to share their eschatological concentration. This was no doubt an unexpected consequence of Paul's treatment of the end as not too remote. It encouraged idleness and even lack of discipline in the church (5:12-13). To live under the threat of the imminent end does not foster Christian charity; it is as difficult to fulfill this duty in the eschatological period as it is in the dull course of history.

What we call the Second Coming is called in biblical studies the *Parousia*. This Greek word designated the ceremonial visit of a monarch to a city, and the Christian community applied it to the return of Jesus Messiah and King. That Paul speaks of "us" in 4:13-18 indicates that he expected to be among the witnesses of this event. In the world which he knew it was not an impossible dream that the gospel should be proclaimed to the whole world (Matthew 24:14). But while this phrase of Matthew can be used to illustrate Paul, we must remember that the epistles of Paul are earlier than any Gospel, and that the form in which Paul expressed his belief in the Parousia is earlier than the eschatological discourses of the Synoptic Gospels. There is no essential contradiction between Paul's belief and the passages of the Gospels, and it is very likely that the belief in the Parousia was one of the Christian beliefs to take form very early. For our purpose here it is sufficient to notice that the eschatological discourses as well as Paul do not seem to suppose a long interval before the Parousia; most of those to whom the words are addressed may expect to be present at the event.

Unless the Thessalonians believed the Parousia was near, their question would have no meaning. Apparently they were more assured of the Parousia than they were of the resurrection, for their worry was about those who had died and therefore could not witness the Parousia. Paul reassures them by affirming the resurrection. The Parousia itself is briefly described in terms of ancient and biblical cosmology;

God dwells in heaven above, and it is from above that the Lord will appear. The elect, both the risen and those who are still living at the moment, will be swept up into midair to meet the Lord. These features are not peculiarly Christian (see the note in the Jerusalem Bible); they are commonplace in Jewish apocalyptic literature, and the clouds and the trumpet of the angel appear in Matthew 24:31.

That Paul expects to see the Parousia does not mean that he wishes to set a time for it. His insistence that it will be sudden and unexpected, just at the moment when things seem peaceful, is echoed in the Synoptic Gospels (Mt 24:37-44; Mk 13:33-37; Lk 21:34). Matthew also has the image of the thief who does not announce his coming. This theme of suddenness is not quite in harmony with II Th and some portions of the Synoptic eschatological discourses (see below). One can prepare for the event only by unfailing vigilance; the life of the Christian is a perpetual daylight of wakefulness. For this unbroken vigil the Christian must stand like a soldier in armor; but the attributes of virtue with which he is armed are partly borrowed from Isaiah 59:17, where they are the armor of God. The sense of urgency which Paul expresses is based on the expectation of the Parousia. When this expectation grew dim, Christianity seemed to discover no other motive for a sense of urgency. Without the Parousia Christianity tends to become an establishment maintaining itself, and not a restless movement forward toward a destiny which is both hoped and feared, but which alone makes sense of the human adventure.

II Thessalonians is more explicit in its purpose to correct a misapprehension. Paul briefly praises the church for the same virtues which he praised in I Th, and in urging them to withstand persecution he appeals to the explicit picture of the Parousia of judgment. This picture is even more candidly mythological than the Parousia of I Th, and the emphasis is upon judgment of unbelief rather than upon the rewards of belief. This gives II Th 1:6-10 a vindictive tone which is not usual in the letters of Paul; vindictiveness is an occupational hazard of a vivid mythology of the last things.

The letter is written principally to correct the belief that the day of the Lord (the day of the Parousia) has arrived. Precisely what shape this error took is difficult to conjecture. As the Parousia is described in Paul and in the Synoptic eschatological discourses, it seems impossible to imagine anyone believing that it had happened without being generally noticed. One consequence of this belief is mentioned in 3:10-12. Other consequences of a belief that the end time had arrived are not mentioned by Paul; among these are the abolition of all or most obligations and the confirmation of the saints in positions of power. The second seems unlikely in the Thessalonian church; the first is simply not mentioned as a real danger.

The passage explaining the signs of the Parousia (2:3-12) is difficult in itself, as we shall show shortly; and those who doubt that Paul wrote the letter point out that an event cannot be sudden and unpredictable and at the same time preceded by recognizable signs. The fact that we do not understand the signs does not mean that Paul and the Thessalonians did not, or did not think they did. We have remarked that the same inconsistency can be seen in the Synoptic eschatological discourses. We have already noted the passages in which the Gospels affirm that the Parousia will be sudden and unexpected. Yet they also say that it will be preceded by signs (Mt 24:32-33); Mk 13:28-29; Lk 21:29-31). The signs of the Gospels are, if possible, more obscure than the signs of Paul. The inconsistency must be granted; at the same time, vivid eschatological beliefs seem to impose a certain inconsistency on those who accept them.

For Paul, the Parousia must be preceded by the great Rebellion and the appearance of the great Rebel, the Enemy; it is generally thought that this is the same eschatological image as the Antichrist (I Jn 2:18; 4:3). Something similar is probably meant by the false Christs of Mt 24:4-5, 23-24, and by the growth of lawlessness and the cooling of love (Mt 24:12). These two signs are now withheld by "that which holds back" (2:5-6). Paul alludes briefly to these, reminding the Thessalonians of the fuller teaching which he had to give them in person. Without the fuller teaching, modern interpreters have been compelled to do a great deal of educated guesswork.

Briefly, the question is whether Paul thought of these signs as historical or typical; that is, whether he viewed the Rebellion and the Rebel as future historical events and a future person or whether they signified trends in history. Most modern interpreters explain them as typical. Earlier interpreters from the Fathers of the church into modern times thought of them as historical, particularly the Enemy. Individual historical interpretation is not recommended by the texts of Matthew, which speak of false Christs in the plural. Perhaps Paul has turned the plural and the general phenomena into the concrete and the particular; or perhaps the interpretation of Matthew has generalized the particular. It seems very likely (although most interpreters do not think so) that Paul regarded the Rebel and the Rebellion as concretely and particularly as he thought of the Parousia of which they were a sign. If they are meant to be concrete and future, then it is useless to think that Paul (or whoever wrote II Th) was using code words for concrete historical persons and events which he knew quite well. And the mention of signs of the Parousia by no means contradicts Paul's expectations of a Parousia in the near future.

Paul sees the history of the church in a single series as progress followed by opposition, which reaches a focus in a single individual. This opposition seems to develop within the church; it is not clearly persecution from enemies which Paul apprehends. This corresponds to the last great cosmic war against the sovereignty of God which is characteristic of Jewish apocalyptic; and it may be significant that Paul thinks this last great resistance will come from within the Christian community masking itself as a Christian phenomenon. Without using the term false Christ it appears that this is what Paul means.

What Paul sees as a single event is from our perspective a forecast of the history of the church—recurrent rebellions within the church and recurrent Rebels and Enemies, "men of sin," produced within the church. In this sense, the typical interpretation is correct over against the historical, but I think that we are restating and modifying what Paul actually said while we preserve what he meant. The major exegetical problem remains the problem of identifying "the Restraint" (2:6-7) which prevents the Rebel from appearing. Many ancient and modern interpreters think of the Roman Empire, which was a principle of order and stability in the world of Paul; how this Restraint was to become ineffective within a generation is not clear. Many modern interpreters renounce any effort to identify the Restraint. One sympathizes with their despair, but one feels that Paul had something definite in mind, something which he thought important. If we cannot find it, it is unimportant to us. Paul sees the Restraint as being removed. It seems that this must be identified in some way with the church rather than with a political or cosmic power. I do not mean that the Restraint is synonymous with the church, but with some aspect of its reality or its operation. The removal of the Restraint, then, is seen to be some failure of the church to fulfill its reality.

This exposition is followed by a rather pedestrian exhortation to persevere (2:13—3:5). And it in turn is followed by a sharp attack on idleness. In fact Paul attacks more than idleness; he is attacking eschatological irresponsibility. Since God alone can act effectively in history, and since he is going to act effectively in a short time by ending history altogether, there is no reason for doing anything, not even for supporting oneself. The vigor of Paul's attack is a little surprising; as we have remarked, this was an unexpected result of eschatologism. Perhaps it should have been expected. Paul does not take the trouble to explain why it is grievously wrong to refuse to carry one's share of the load, whether for an imminent Parousia or for anything else. A community of love is based first of all on the supposition that everyone does all he can and all he ought. This is the basic duty of love which we rarely think of as a work of love. One has little difficulty in sharing Paul's criticism of the freeloaders, as we would call them nowadays. No work, no food; it is not a solution to the problem which many would dare recommend in our own context. Some might wonder whether it is a Christian solution at all.

Chapter Three
EPISTLE TO THE GALATIANS

This is the earliest of the four "great" epistles (with I-II Corinthians, Romans). The adjective refers in the first place to the length of the epistles, but it also recognizes that the four letters are the most important in their doctrine. The address raises questions which present no problem for most readers. In the time of Paul, Galatia was a Roman province (and had been since 24 B.C.) in Anatolia, the plateau in the central part of Asia Minor. The province had been expanded by the incorporation of districts to which the original name Galatia did not apply; the name designated a kingdom formed by tribes which had emmigrated from Gaul in the third century. Acts refers to missionary work of Paul in the districts added to Galatia (16:1-6, 18:23); while a journey through Galatia proper is mentioned, no church there is mentioned by name. The question is whether the letter is addressed to the churches mentioned in Acts or to others in northern Galatia. The question has not been settled and does not affect the interpretation of the epistle. Ancient Galatia, like modern Anatolia, lay somewhat off the mainstreams of traffic and of culture. The people were peasants and mountaineers, and parts of the territory were infested by bandits.

The letter begins more abruptly than any other letter of Paul. It is occasioned by a church problem which causes him personal anxiety, and Paul makes no attempt to ease his way into the rebuke which he must write. The thanksgiving with which the other letters open is omitted. This does not keep Paul from reaching a personal and affectionate tone before the letter is ended. Critics are accustomed to say that if Paul did not write this letter he did not write any; a personality emerges, in spite of the brevity of the letter, the same personality who is recognized in the undoubted letters of Paul.

The letter was written in response to a situation created by troublemakers. They were known both to Paul and to the Galatians, so he does not identify them or state their position or the charges against him which they must have made. They are identified with those whom we call "Judaizers." We shall meet this group in several other letters, but their character never emerges clearly. Paul's caution in avoiding names may suggest that they included some important people in the infant church. In the first decades of the church it appeared to the Roman authorities and probably to most converts, whether Jews or Gentiles, as a sect of Judaism. The word Christian means "messianist," one who believes that the Messiah has come. Of itself such a belief does not separate one from Judaism. Other elements of belief did cause separation, and most of them are mentioned here. However, our point is that the early church was Jewish in most of its membership and in most of its worship, and it had no religious literature except the sacred books of the Jews. To say that these adversaries were Jewish Christians is to say nothing about them; to say that they were Jews who added to Judaism the belief that the Messiah had come is not to add much. They brought into the open certain implications of their belief. It seems that Paul had rejected these implications in his proclamations without explicitly recognizing it. The Judaizers compelled him to take more advanced positions, which have their earliest written formulation in Galatians. They are more fully formulated in later letters, particularly to Romans. The reader of the epistles should recognize the relations between Galatians and Romans.

Since the position of the Judaizers is nowhere set forth, we have no reason to think that it was one consistent position. Some recent scholars have suggested that they were Gentile Christians who were more Jewish than the original disciples; one is reminded of our description of converts who wish to be more Catholic than the Pope. They seem to have gone from the fact that the first believers were Jews who became Christians to the principle that all who became Christians had to become Jews first. They may, as some have suggested, have presented Jewish Christianity not as an absolute demand but as required for perfect Christianity; but Paul makes no such distinction. He mentions circumcision, the rite which makes a man a Jew. No woman was a Jew; she was the daughter or the wife of a Jew. He mentions the observance of the Law, but it is not certain that the Judaizers insisted on its full observance. The Judaizers were the first in a long and uninterrupted line of Christians who taught that for sure or perfect Christianity something more than what Jesus taught was required.

Paul opens his response with an affirmation of the authenticity of his call to the apostolate. To a modern reader it seems strange that he appeals to a different revelation of Jesus Christ and insists that he did not learn his gospel from any of the original disciples. In the modern church this claim would certainly prove that he was a false apostle. We would demand credentials from church authorities. For this, among other reasons, scholars believe that the early church defined an apostle as one who had received a personal commission from Jesus to proclaim the gospel throughout the whole world. Paul had his gospel years before he discussed it with the "pillars" of Jerusalem; but just as he had not learned his gospel from them, so he admits no right of theirs to pass judgment on his gospel. He admits somewhat grudgingly and for the sake of the Galatians that they found no fault in his gospel, and they accepted his apostolic commission to preach to the Gentiles as Peter was commissioned to preach to the Jews (outside Palestine).

Paul found the actions of Peter (whom he prefers to call by the Aramaic form of the name, Cephas) inconsistent with his acceptance of Paul's gospel. The fact that Peter is said to have acted out of fear is an indication that the Judaizers included important people. Denial of table fellowship was what later became excommunication; this implication was not realized. Paul's gospel, which he summarizes briefly in 2:15-21, was that faith in Christ is required and sufficient for righteousness. The believer dies with Christ (and for the Jew this meant the end of his life as a Jew) and begins a new life, the life of Christ who lives in him. If the Law makes one righteous, then there was nothing which the death of Christ could accomplish. This simple summary has vast implications, not all of which are worked out in this epistle.

Paul supports his gospel by biblical arguments; and the rabbinical character of his arguments makes us wonder whether he was addressing Jewish or Gentile Christians. The probability is that they were Gentiles, and we must suppose that Paul and the other apostles acquainted them with the Jewish Scriptures. Abraham was righteous; this could not have been righteousness of Law, for it did not yet exist. So it was righteousness of faith; and because of his faith a blessing was promised to all nations who share in that faith. The faith of the promise is contrasted to the curse which is laid upon those who violate the Law. Arguing as from the law of legacy, Paul treats the promise as a last will and testament which is not canceled by a codicil. The argument, we said, is rabbinical; and one who works his way through it will have a good idea of what this term means.

Here in Galatians Paul encounters a problem which is never entirely solved; for both the Law and the promise are revelations of the will of God, and Paul is compelled to choose between the promise and the Law. It is resolved only by taking the Law as a temporary and imperfect disposition which yields to fulfillment of the promise. The appeal to the fatherhood of God and sonship of the believers is important in the argument, and the belief is found in the Gospels. Paul could not quote them because they had not yet been written. The father does not govern his sons by law. Hence the Law was imposed as a restraint upon sin until the promise was fulfilled. All the Law could do was restrain sin, and Paul denies (more explicitly in Romans) that the Law succeeded even in this.

Paul compares the Law to slavery—or better, to the condition of the child. Actually in Roman law, which Paul is probably thinking of, the child was a chattel over whom the father had the same rights he had over his slaves. The Law was like the "pedagogue," the slave who took the child to school. When the child reaches his majority, he is free. The validity of the argument depends on two principles; that God is a father, and that the Law is no more than a restraint on sin. A further conclusion which Paul merely touches on is that the unity of the believers creates a single family under one father. The church has not yet reached a unity in which differences as deep as those between Jew and Greek, slave and free, and male and female are less important than the unity. Paul has no revolutionary program for the society he knew, but he states the principles by which that society can be changed.

Paul mentions slavery to "the elemental principles of this world" (4:3, 9); what he meant by this is a problem, and no reference is found in contemporary Judaism to which it can be referred. There are indications, however, that Paul shared the popular belief in spiritual cosmic powers (Eph 1:21; 3:10; 6:12); these he considered the realities behind idols as well as the powers which supported worldly political power. If this is what he meant, then Paul obliquely calls the observance of the Law the same as devil worship. This would be strong medicine, and it is odd that he is explicit in this context only about the observances of sacred festivals and seasons.

Almost as an afterthought, and surely without much attention to the order of logic or of rhetoric, Paul adds the biblical argument from Hagar and Sarah as the allegory of the two covenants. One wonders whether the Galatians found this passage as obscure as modern congregations do. According to a law now known as widely practiced in the ancient Near East 1500 years before Christ, the barren wife could furnish one of her slaves as a substitute wife. If the slave bore a son, he had full standing as a son and if he was first-born had all the rights of the first-born unless the wife herself later bore a son. The slave could not be reduced to slavery nor expelled. Paul knew nothing of this law. Ishmael, the son of Hagar, was a son of Abraham according to the flesh as much as Isaac was; but Isaac was the son who had been promised. Thus mere carnal descent from Abraham, while it does not imply slavery, does not exclude it; but the promise is what confers freedom. The association of Sinai in Arabia with Hagar the Arabian is somewhat gratuitously added; and the association of Sarah with the heavenly Jerusalem is based on nothing in the text. The reader who wishes to know what midrash is can learn by studying this passage carefully. Midrash draws an inspirational or a practical conclusion from the text of the Bible by attributing value to every word and to every possible verbal association.

The last two chapters have caused some interpreters to wonder whether Paul did not have a double purpose in mind. To urge the abolition of the Law with no law to replace it can be taken as a denial of any obligation, and it has been so taken more than once in the history of Christianity. Paul repeats his emphatic statement of freedom (5:1-12) and his emphasis carries him so far that he practically makes the Law an obstacle to virtue rather than a help; the problem of the implications of this statement recurs in Romans. It also leads him to a gibe at the Judaizers which is more crude by modern standards (5:12) than it was in the first century.

Paul reduces the entire Law to the commandment of love (5:14). This summary recurs in Romans 13:9; again, although Paul could not quote the Gospels, the same teaching is found in a saying of Jesus (Mark 12:28-34; Matthew 22:34-40; Luke 10:25-28). Both the Law and the commandment of love are opposed to "self-indulgence." The Law, as Paul explains more fully in Romans, opposes self-indulgence but presents no effective means of restraint. Self-indulgence is opposed effectively only by the Spirit, which raises man above both self-indulgence and the Law. According to a literary technique of Hellenistic rhetoric and philosophy Paul presents two opposed catalogues of virtues and vices. The two are not formally opposed point by point, and they are not balanced in number; in fact the celebrated twelve fruits of the Holy Spirit are only nine in the critical Greek texts. The nine are, with the possible exception of the ninth, synonyms and variations of love. The catalogue of vices is wider in scope. This fact—that love and the virtues are the fruits of the Spirit, expelling all varieties of vicious conduct—implies a point which Paul makes explicit in other letters; Christian love, which is the fulfillment of the whole Law, is a charismatic work, impossible without the indwelling Spirit, and therefore impossible to the Jew who has not believed in the Messiah. The modern reader may again feel a twinge of discomfort at the confidence which Paul places in the guidance of the Spirit, seeing here ample room for deception of self and of others and even for horrors done in the name of the guidance of the Spirit. Paul's confidence in the Spirit was not misplaced, but even he did not perceive to what purposes men could turn the gospel. For Paul the Spirit is love, and he does not seem to think it possible to make a mistake if one is guided by love. We have had to modify this principle, not always to advantage.

Chapter 6, the conclusion of which (11-18) was written in Paul's own hand, has to be judged as rambling. The emphasis is placed on love, on the works of love, and on directions for the petty details of daily life in which men most easily fail to show love for each other. Paul is not asking for heroic feats, unless the maintaining of love in a routine is a heroic feat. He might say that if you can die for another, you can at least forgive him.

The epilogue, Paul's autograph, could almost be taken as the beginning of another letter. We shall meet the theme of the cross later in other letters; Paul introduced this theme into Christian theology and spirituality, and he does it here quite abruptly. What has become the Christian badge of honor was, when Paul wrote, the instrument of capital punishment reserved for slaves and particularly antisocial crimes such as treason (with which Jesus was charged), piracy and armed robbery. The dignity of the Roman citizen was preserved even if he fell foul of the law; gentlemen were beheaded. It is difficult for the modern reader to appreciate the extravagance of Paul's statement that his only boast is the cross of Christ. Paul accepts the cross as the symbol of his separation from the world, by which he means in this context the wealth and pomp and power which are so often associated with "the world." Not that Paul had any reason to hope for wealth and pomp and power, or that he thought he was effectively renouncing them; he means that he is willing to accept the contempt of the world of wealth and power which that world shows to the lowest members of society, those members on whom it inflicted the penalty of the cross. This is a theme to which Paul returns at greater length in I-II Corinthians. The boast of the cross is opposed to the boasts of the Judaizers, circumcision and the Law; and the modern reader must realize that this was a boast. Jews thought themselves infinitely superior to pagans in morality; and while their pride was exaggerated, it was not unfounded. Against this boast Paul proposes a new life, a new creation; the theme of death and resurrection into a new life in Christ is a recurrent theme in other epistles.

The sharpness of the letter is preserved in 6:17, the next to the last sentence. One can only wonder at the highly personal tone which lies between the beginning and the end, both of which exhibit sharpness. We see what we have said in the introduction, that these are letters, truly personal communications, and not doctrinal treatises.

Chapter Four

FIRST EPISTLE TO THE CORINTHIANS

The ancient Greek city of Corinth lay on the isthmus of Corinth, the narrow land strip (four miles wide) which joined the Peloponnesus to the mainland of Greece. Corinth had been destroyed by the Romans in 146 B.C. and refounded by Julius Caesar in 44 B.C. Its situation on the isthmus, where goods and even small ships were transported by land to shorten the east-west voyage on the Mediterranean, had made Corinth a large and prosperous city by A.D. 50, when Paul founded a church there. The mission was not too promising; Corinth was celebrated as a center of prostitution.

The two letters are not the entire correspondence of Paul to Corinth. A letter earlier than I Corinthians is mentioned (I Cor. 5:9-11), and II Corinthians presents problems of its own to be discussed later. There were at least two letters from members of the Corinthian church to Paul. Both I-II Corinthians were clearly responses to troubles in the church of Corinth; Paul had been informed of these difficulties by letters, by members of his own staff, and finally by visitors from the church of Corinth (I Cor 1:11; 16:15-18). Furthermore, both I and II Corinthians should probably be dated in A.D. 57—I Cor in the spring and II Cor in the fall.

The introduction (1:1-9) is neither remarkably long nor remarkably short; and while the wishes for grace and peace seem appropriate for the letter which follows, this is a standard phrase in the introductions to all the letters. Paul plunges directly into what he takes as the most urgent problem, the existence of parties or factions in the church. What he and the Corinthians understood very well has worried modern interpreters a great deal; we do not know on what the parties differed and of what significance were the personal names attached to the parties. But as far as we know, Peter (Cephas) had never been to Corinth. Apollos, as Paul makes clear in the text, was in no way a rival of Paul or a cause of dissension. The party of "Christ" suggests the self-appointed elite groups which the church has known so often and still knows. It seems clear that, unless Paul is being discreet to a degree which he never attains elsewhere, these parties were not as serious a threat to Christian unity as the Judaizing party against which Galatians was written. The problem is discussed in 1:10—4:21, and to complete the treatment Paul discusses both Christian teaching and the Christian apostle-teacher. Paul's treatment in no way indicates that the parties were divided over doctrine.

The antithesis between true wisdom and false wisdom (1:7—3:4) suggests that some Corinthians found the gospel too simple and wished to enrich it with human knowledge (wisdom is rendered by the JB, not too accurately, as "philosophy"). Certainly doctrine in the church has been involved with human learning (which has not always meant enrichment) since the third century. Clearly Paul had no use for it, and possibly this rejection of Greek learning reflects his rabbinical background. One may judge that the congregation was not ready for this type of sophistication; and Paul's extremely frank appraisal of the Corinthians (1:26) ranks them as lacking the education which was required for a "learned" faith. Having granted all this, the dominant theme of Paul's exposition is his statement that the gospel is a frontal challenge to human wisdom and human power. Human wisdom cannot devise a plan of redemption through the cross. The believer is taught not by human learning but by the spirit of God. The Corinthians have not yet been taught by the Spirit, and Paul tells them that they simply have not grown up enough to discuss these questions.

The gospel is Christ, and Christ is the power and the wisdom of God. This is the earliest New Testament statement of the gospel as the word of power which needs nothing from any other human resource. The apostle can only and need only proclaim it, and the mere proclamation brings the listener to the crisis of faith. It is in the terms of this word of power that Paul wishes the Corinthians to understand the apostle and his mission. The apostles are merely servants, like the slave who sets the food on the table. They are the farmers who plant and water, but must wait for another power to produce growth. By another figure, Paul likens himself to the architect of the church of Corinth, but this is merely because he was its founder. The church is a building which must be completed by others besides the architect. Paul almost forgets this figure in 4:14-17 below, where he likens himself, as founder, to the father of a family; this affords him a peculiar relationship to the church of Corinth which is hardly the same as the relation of the architect to the completed building. The work of the builder will be tested by fire, which can hardly be anything but the test of temptation and suffering. The work will stand if it is the gospel; human learning and human eloquence will fall. Almost as an afterthought Paul identifies the building not with the church but with the individual Christian, a theme to which he returns in 6:19. Unlike Jews and pagans, Christians had no temple or holy place, just as they had no priests; consequently, the ancient category of the "holy" receives a new definition in the gospel.

Since the apostle is merely a servant and a steward, he is to be judged by the virtue of the steward, which is fidelity to his charge. Paul insists that both he and Apollos have been faithful. Now Paul asks, not without sarcasm, how the Corinthians have learned to judge apostles—returning to the factions—since they have no gospel other than the one, and only one, gospel which the men whose names they bandy about as slogans have proclaimed to them.

The impoverishment and suffering of the apostolic mission have rendered the apostles contemptible—"the scum of the earth"—while the Corinthians, like kings, sit in judgment on the men from whom they have learned everything they know.

Yet in spite of the sarcasm, which cuts deeply, Paul's

defense is strangely moderate and humble, ending with the appeal, already noticed, to the human relationship which was created between the apostle and his disciples. But Paul has other resources, which he calls the stick in his hand. He seems to signify no more than rebuke strengthened by personal presence and confrontation. That the stick did not instantly quell dissension is evident from some of the things stated in II Corinthians.

One can see from the outline and paragraph heading in the JB that next Paul takes up three more problems which had been reported to him (chapters 5-6). It is not clear that the topics treated in chapters 11-15 were proposed as questions; some reports about Corinthian practices were mentioned, but the treatment is broader than any questions stated or implied in the text. In all these topics, as in the question of factions, what makes Paul's treatment of archaic problems permanently valuable is the depth of the theological background from which he responds to the questions.

The first case (5:1-13) is a case of incest—the marriage (although Paul refuses to use the word) of a man with his stepmother, prohibited both in Jewish and Roman law. Possibly it was tolerated because the man was a Jewish proselyte, and in rabbinical theory circumcision was a legal death which terminated all existing relationships and obligations. More interesting is the view that the man applied to himself the theory of baptism as a death and rebirth, an interpretation which Paul himself proposed, possibly in relation to the rabbinical understanding of circumcision. Paul certainly rejects this view implicitly in this connection. The sentence uttered is excommunication, which is delivery to damnation for one who is baptized. The purpose of the sentence, however, is medicinal, not punitive; it is hoped that the man will repent. The community protects itself from temptation by expelling such unworthy members; this much it must do, although Paul realistically does not expect Christians to avoid temptation by withdrawing from the world.

Paul handles lawsuits between Christians with what a modern reader finds surprising insistence. The "unjust" (6:1) represent the Hebrew word "unrighteous," not made righteous in Christ; the Greek permits the word play. The "unrighteous" can hardly be trusted to administer "justice." The English translation fails to make it clear that the same word appears in 6:9 as "wrongdoers." Suits in a court of law exhibit a hostility between the contending parties which Paul believes should not exist between Christians. Christians should be able to settle their differences privately; the same teaching occurs in Matthew 18:15-17. They should even be willing to risk a loss rather than a quarrel (see Matthew 5:38-48). Paul's statement that the believers will judge the world and even angels (6:2-3) reflects the same eschatological image as that which appears in Matthew 19:28; Luke 22:28-30; Revelation 20:4. The rejection of the "unrighteous" is repeated with even more emphasis, and it seems with unnecessary harshness. Paul somewhat overstates his case in arguing that those who are completely outside the kingdom can contribute nothing to believers; and he reminds the Corinthians that they themselves are not long removed from the condition of unrighteousness.

It is probably mere loose association with the recital of vices in 6:9 that leads Paul to say a few words directed at the most notorious vice of Corinth. What ancient sources tell us about Corinth, known as a debauched city even in the easy life of the Roman Empire, compels us to wonder at Paul's restraint; many more recent preachers would have devoted the entire letter to this topic. The normal adult male in the Hellenistic-Roman cities thought no more of dropping in at the neighborhood brothel than he did of visiting the public baths; there was absolutely no ethical consideration involved in either, and both contributed to a healthy body and a balanced mind. Paul's argument here is the theme already mentioned (3:17) that the body of the believer is the temple of God. He assumes that his listeners know that a person cannot be one body with a prostitute and one spirit with God.

Paul's discussion of marriage and virginity (chapter 7) is much quoted and discussed, and it is still not entirely clear. Paul approves marriage, and insists on its permanence and on fidelity to its obligations. Apparently there had been some question about this, and we shall return to this question below. The exception is "the Pauline privilege" (vv. 12-16). The believer who separates may marry; "the brother or sister is not tied" can mean nothing else. What Paul allows is divorce in this case. The church has not seen fit to extend the principle "God has called you to a life of peace" to other cases in which one partner does not consent to cohabit but "departs" (the English does not bring out this word in v. 15).

Apart from this case, Paul recommends no effort to change one's condition—married or single, slave or free, circumcised or uncircumcised. The reason for this is eschatological urgency (vv. 29-31); "the passing world" means that Paul does not expect much time before the Parousia and the consummation, as we noticed in I-II Thessalonians. One may ask whether the recommendation retains its validity if the eschatological urgency is removed, and, of course, one is answered that the day of the Lord still comes like a thief in the night. It remains true that a Christian who chose his state in life in A.D. 57 on the hypothesis that the day of the Lord would come by A.D. 65 may have chosen correctly, but not on a correct assumption. That one should treat the world as passing is sound Christian asceticism; but we have already (in treating I-II Thessalonians) referred to eschatological irresponsibility.

In the remaining sections of the chapter, Paul expresses a theme in which celibacy—and here he means not merely abstinence from marriage, but abstinence from sex—is preferred to marriage. It is not attached to professional dedication to the church; Paul says he would like all to be as he is. Many interpreters believe that Paul, who was an adult and a rabbi at his conversion, must have been a widower; the rabbis had no use or sympathy for celibacy. That Paul's doctrine has endured in Catholic teaching needs no demonstration or comment; for the interpreter, the problem is simply one of the course of Paul's teaching here. Paul is earlier than any of the Gospels; but even if the possible allusions to celibacy in the Gospel are taken at their full possible value, they are not at all as lengthy and explicit as the words of this chapter. Paul's teaching cannot be clearly traced back to the teaching of Jesus. The reader of this chapter will notice that Paul is unusually careful to distinguish between the teaching of the Lord (on the permanence of marriage, for instance) and his own recommendations (the Pauline privilege, for instance). Paul says expressly (v. 25) that he has no directions from the Lord concerning celibacy. One is nearly compelled to the conclusion that the teaching on celibacy as an ideal is original with Paul. One is not so rigorously moved to conclude that his teaching on celibacy follows from the eschatological urgency mentioned above; but it is hardly fair to leave this factor out of the interpretation of his teaching altogether.

The JB by its translation of 7:36-38 adopted one side of an ancient and celebrated exegetical dispute concerning the identity of the man in these verses. The JB understands him to be the father of the maiden. In Jewish and Roman law the choice of a husband lay with the father of the bride. Paul in this interpretation extends this paternal power to the decision of whether the girl should marry at all, and he expresses his own ideal of celibacy. It seems that this understanding strengthens the view that Paul speaks from eschatological urgency; a general and permanent recommendation that fathers should not give their daughters in marriage seems most improbable. To the modern reader this paternal power over a daughter seems revolting. To Paul and his listeners it was a social disposition in accord with nature. One should not conclude, however, that Paul has nothing at all of value to say to the modern world on sex and marriage. Clearly he has nothing to say to the modern world on how a father should make decisions concerning the marriage of his daughter.

The question of eating meat sacrificed to idols is treated at a length which surprises the modern reader. It was a practical question of human relations. Most of the meat sacrificed to gods in the temples was not consumed in the sacrifice; what was left over belonged to the priests, and what they did not use themselves was sold to butchers for sale to the public.

The Christian worried whether his eating of consecrated meat was participation in the cult of the gods. Furthermore, much of the social life of the ancient world revolved around family festivals. These often had a religious tone; not only was the meat likely to be sacrificial, but the dinner itself was often held in a temple. Most of the new Christians had friends and relatives who were pagans—that is, the "wrongdoers" of 6:9. Paul did not want Christians to go into lawcourts before the unrighteous, but he certainly did not forbid the amenities toward old friends or relatives; and this breadth has not always been respected by Christians.

The basic solution (chapter 8) is simple. Since an idol is not a reality, it is impossible to worship it for those who know this. They may treat the idol as nonexistent; food cannot be consecrated to it. But there is a restraint on this freedom; this is what has become known in theology as "the scandal of the weak." One who in ignorance thinks that your action is wrong may follow your example against his own conscience. There is some inconsistency in Paul's thesis; for one way in which the erroneous conscience becomes informed is by the example of those whose consciences are correct. Whether Paul noticed this or not, he did not care about it. It is the duty of the knowledgeable and strong person to adjust himself to the weak, not the duty of the weak to yield to the strong.

Paul thought that this principle was difficult enough to deserve an extended illustration—more extended than the statement of the principle itself (chapter 9). Paul illustrates from his own apostolate; the office gives him rights which he has not urged. The rights extend to support by contributions from the churches and to traveling with a female companion. Paul was a tentmaker (Acts 18:3); through his trade he made the acquaintance of Aquila and Priscilla. He argues vigorously for the right to live by the gospel, which he did not exercise lest it be a hindrance to the mission. From this point he launches by digression into his duty to proclaim the gospel and the lengths to which he is ready to go in order to adjust his way of life to those to whom he preaches. He compares his dedication to that of the competitive athlete. Rarely has anyone proposed more earnestly that a good work is its own reward. Yet the conclusion is inescapable that Paul was a full-time tentmaker and a part-time apostle. This is less disturbing than it sounds. If he was preaching to the working men of Corinth, he could hardly have done much of it during working hours. The analogy between Paul's style of apostleship and the "worker priests" of recent times is evident. Paul, like the modern worker priests, had to apologize for his departure from what early became a conventional apostolic style.

We have used the ambiguous phrase "female companion" for the second apostolic privilege which Paul renounced. Strangely, the Greek language had no word for "wife," and in this context "woman" is ambiguous. It is thought that most of the Twelve and the other apostles, who were normal men, were married, but it is asserted only of Peter. The explicit inclusion of the wife in the apostolic renunciations is found in the Synoptic Gospels only in Luke 18:29. Paul, as we have mentioned, was probably a widower, and he has already set forth his reasons for remaining single. Hence it seems unlikely that his privilege means simply the right to marry, but rather to travel with a woman who took care of the personal needs of the apostle.

Paul returns to his case (10:1-13) with a brief warning based on biblical traditions against those who have dangerous "knowledge" which gives self-importance (8:1). From this he introduces a new element into the discussion (10:14-22). Participation in social events should not become actual participation in the cult. Actually Paul's first statements seem to have been written without any thinking on this problem. The Eucharist is the Christian feast which excludes any share in the festival cults of false gods. The allusion to the one body symbolized by the one loaf (10:17) seems to set the Christians apart as a distinct cultic group. In conclusion, Paul permits the eating of meat sold in public markets and of food served at social events. But if one of the "weak" asks a question, out of love for him one should abstain. Give glory to God and avoid offense—it is a sound principle, if not always an illuminating guide in practice.

Chapters 11-14 deal with problems of worship, and in particular with those gifts called charismata (12-14).Paul's insistence on the veiling of women has been the basis of a long ecclesiastical tradition, but the theological basis for his assertion is far from firm. The argument that man is the head of the woman is not sympathetic to modern readers as a reflection of ancient culture. The reference to the angels may imply that angels were believed to be present at worship; but why should women veil for them? Some see an allusion to the myth of the concupiscent angels derived from Gen 6:1-4. It remains probable, when Paul's vigorous language is considered, that the prostitutes of Corinth were recognized by their unveiled heads and bobbed hair. The language of 11:13-15 suggests that Paul did not wear the long hair and beard of traditional art, but wore the short haircut and the clean shave of the Roman gentlemen portrayed in contemporary art.

Paul's admonitions on the Eucharist (11:17-34) contain the earliest formula of institutions; it is closer to Luke than to Mark-Matthew, and all the formulas are thought to come from the liturgy. The Eucharist was preceded by a social dinner of the community; Paul complains that this was not an effective symbol of unity. While there may have been many causes of unworthiness, disunity is the only cause to which Paul directs this passage. As in 10:17, the Eucharist is viewed primarily as a sacramental sign of unity; the sign can be rendered ineffective by disunity.

The spiritual gifts (*charismata*), as it becomes evident in the subsequent discussion, are movements of the Spirit which empower the recipients to perform extraordinary actions. These extraordinary actions are still cultivated in the modern pentecostal churches—and now by some groups of Catholics. In strict pentecostal belief only the gifts prove the presence of the Spirit in the community. The analysis of these phenomena is a complex theological and psychological process for which no space is available here. But Paul first asserts that the most elementary act of faith, the profession of faith that Jesus is Lord, cannot be made except under the charismatic action of the Spirit; he is not interested in supporting the attraction of the Corinthians for the bizarre and exotic.

The gifts enumerated in 12:7-10 are not all "extraordinary" as we would understand the word; several of them are "official" in the modern church. Paul makes it clear that any service of the church or any function within the church, whether official or occasional, cannot be done without the power of the Spirit—meaning that it is charismatic. This belief is now expressed in the liturgy of the sacraments, in which the Spirit is ritually conferred for membership and adulthood (baptism and confirmation), liturgical office (orders) and death (anointing of the sick). Paul's treatment is directed against the vanity which could arise from the possession of a more eminent (or more spectacular) gift. The gifts are from the one Spirit and they appear in the one body. The Spirit is no less active in the humbler gifts, and the body is no less active in the humbler gifts, and the body has need both of the more eminent and of the more humble gifts. It is a clear statement of the social democracy of the church.

Again, almost as an afterthought, Paul speaks of the supreme charisms without which the others are worthless (chapter 13). Love is the first and fundamental duty of every Christian, the act which is the fulfillment of the whole Law. This universal duty is the supreme operation of the spirit within the church, and it is the only gift which endures into the eschatological age. Commentators generally despair of adding any light to this luminous passage; it is that commentary on the first and greatest commandment which makes all other commentary unnecessary.

The gift of tongues (14:1-25) exercised a peculiar fascination. A "strange tongue" could be unintelligible babbling. It is plain that while Paul respects this manifestation, he does not see much use in unintelligible speech; it can easily become vain display. Such stunts as speaking in tongues were intended to impress the unbelievers. Precisely what Paul meant by "prophecy" is not clear; it was certainly thought to be inspired speech, "the word of the Lord" as spoken by the prophets of the Old Testament.

Certainly Paul regulates the gifts at Corinth. It is overwhelming to imagine or envision the worship of the church of Corinth, in which everybody was speaking at once, many in unintelligible shouts. Did Paul know that his regulation was fatal to the charismata? One inspired by the Spirit to speak cannot stand in line while others who have the same Spirit take their turns. In particular, one who is inspired to speak in a strange tongue, if he must have an interpreter present, will remain forever silent. We would like to know the effect of Paul's rules; for it is a safe general assertion that the charismatic speaker is incompatible with rules.

Paul's antifeminism recurs when he forbids women to speak in the church, a rule which is still resented. It does the interpreter little good to point out that Paul reflects an archaic Jewish cultural pattern; such a pattern should not be imposed permanently on Christians. Nor does it help to point out that known examples of pagan priestesses and prophetesses could have strengthened Paul's purpose; one does not make rules for the exceptional. But it should be recognized that he is not making an eternal ordinance.

It is worth noticing that the discussion of the resurrection (chapter 15) is the longest sustained treatment of this topic in the New Testament. The denial of the resurrection may have been influenced by Platonism, which taught that man is a spirit encumbered with a body from which liberation is salvation. Paul appeals to what is probably a creedal formula (vv. 3-4), to the witness of the Twelve and others, and to his own personal experience. The basic fact is the resurrection of Christ, for there is no hope except of resurrection in him and with him. Christ is not established as Lord by the Father unless he overcomes the last and most implacable enemy of man, death. In Romans, as we shall see, Sin-Death are coupled as the synthesis of Evil.

Paul's allusion to "baptism for the dead" is unexplained; probably it was baptism conferred on those who stood as substitutes for catechumens who had died before baptism. In the now traditional theology and liturgy of baptism this practice would be impossible. Is Paul's discussion of the risen body (vv. 35-53) something of a concession to Platonism? In later theological controversies the church insisted much on resurrection of "this body." This is certainly not Paul's insistence. The difference in the risen body is at least that it is immortal and incorruptible.

What does this resurrection of the body involve? Paul does not hesitate to use analogies (called by medieval philosophers "quintessential," i.e., composed of the fifth element). Perhaps more daring is the comparison between the seed and the full grown plant; this would permit the risen body to look literally like nothing human. It is not the only example of Paul's overstatement of a case. But if he did not think of the resurrection as being a transformation, he chose very poor language. The resurrection is not the restoration of that life which ended in death, but a new life. Adam was earthy and "ensouled"; the risen in Christ are heavenly and "inspirited." The risen man is not "flesh and blood," the common biblical term for man in his historical existence; it implies both physical and moral corruptibility. Paul insists upon the transformation, but wisely refrains from any details. Concerning the new life conferred in the resurrection, man has no knowledge and no experience; consequently he has no language for it.

The conclusion (chapter 16) is a typically Pauline conclusion—scattered and disorganized, a mixture of instructions, greetings and admonitions. The collection is mentioned also in Romans, Galatians, and II Corinthians. This massive enterprise was an effort to gather funds in the Gentile churches (certainly of Greece and Rome, possibly also of Asia) for the church of Jerusalem (and of Palestine), which was in severe need due to a famine. The collection seems to imply (as will be indicated in II Corinthians) that the Gentile congregations were better endowed with worldly goods than the Palestinian church. Yet nothing indicates that there were many rich among them. It is possible that Jewish hostility to the messianists achieved a form of economic harassment in Palestine which was impossible in the Gentile cities. For Paul (again, this will appear in II Corinthians), the collection was a means of unifying the "world" church in a community of active love.

Chapter Five
SECOND EPISTLE TO THE CORINTHIANS

It was noted that II Cor followed I Cor by about six months. Unfortunately, details about this period are very sketchy, and the events are important for understanding the epistles. Paul wrote a sorrowful letter (2:3-4) and very probably made a visit to Corinth which was not successful in settling the troubles there—the visit which must be presupposed if Paul decided not to make a "second" distressing visit (2:1). Instead, he sent Titus, who either composed affairs or found them composed, and this enabled Paul to write II Cor in joy. The joy was moderated by factors which will appear below; some commentators have noticed that Paul begins the letter not with a thanksgiving but with a blessing.

That Paul is the author is not questioned, but a number of scholars have wondered whether it is a letter. There are reasons for doubting whether 6:14-17 and chapters 10-13 belong to the letter; the reasons will be mentioned when these passages are discussed. Chapter 9 appears to be a duplicate of chapter 8. For practical reasons as well as because of the majority opinion of scholars we treat the letter as a single work. As such it illustrates, better than any other epistle, Paul's tendency to wander. A possible explanation is that the dictation of the epistle was prolonged over several weeks during a period of obvious tension, at which time, information may have come that altered Paul's ideas and mood.

We noticed that the first topic treated in I Cor was the apostolate, and it is treated at some length. This is also the main topic in II Cor 2:12—6:10 and chapters 10-13. The difference between these two treatments is plain; the second is explicitly defensive. Paul is responding to charges, and these do not come from the factions within the church of Corinth. They come from unidentified persons who have visited Corinth, called "arch-apostles" (11-5) and "counterfeit apostles" (11-13). They were probably Judaizing Christians (11-22), Paul's principal adversaries; and it is possible that they had a rank and importance in the church greater than most commentators have been willing to recognize. It is also possible that the apostolic church was nearer to schism than it has reported in its documents.

The introduction (1:1-11) is a not too delicate hint that the Corinthians have added pain to a life which was amply endowed with suffering from other quarters. Paul immediately turns to the defense of his dealings with Corinth during recent months. His sending of Titus must have been a change from an original declared intention to come himself; thus, his critics, who seem to have been extremely active, took the opportunity to remark that Paul, in addition to other faults, was vacillating. The visit he made was painful; Paul probably spared no words, but he seems to have had no success in restoring peace. "The offender" is mentioned as a single person; he is not named, which may indicate that he was a person of some importance. Ultimately the community rejected the offender and punished him in some way. Paul, however, is ready to forgive; furthermore, he asks that the Corinthians do the same.

Paul begins his discussion of the apostolate (2:12ff) by referring to the anxiety he felt while awaiting Titus' return from Corinth; but again, he immediately falls into a controversy about those who peddle the word of God—which seems to mean that they make money on it. He does not show the same caution which he showed in I Cor 9 concerning the freedom of apostles to live by the gospel; and it is doubtful that conditions had changed notably in six months. Even in the most peaceful parts of II Cor Paul writes with a smoldering resentment. He then alludes to a charge which is not specified: Either he is praising himself, or he does not have the proper letters of recommendation—from Jerusalem, presumably. He responds that the church of Corinth is his recommendation—a delicate way of praising their authentic Christianity.

Paul then compares the new covenant with the old and the apostle with Moses (3:4—4:6). This section was certainly written with the Judaizing Christians in mind, and its ideas are expressed at greater length in Galatians and Romans. The controversial tone here is not vigorous; but it goes far beyond what a Jew would tolerate. The terms of the contrast are letter-spirit, death-life, condemnation-justification, slavery-freedom. By a midrashic interpretation the veil which Moses wore concealed not the brightness which sight could not bear but the fact that the brightness was fading. The veil is now worn by unbelieving Jews, and it shuts out the light of the gospel. Paul very nearly approaches the antithesis of light-darkness, and possibly out of conscious respect for the faith of his fathers he does not employ it. Paul also avoids a direct comparison between the apostle (himself) and Moses; while Paul has moved far from Judaism, this would be too offensive for the Jews or for him. The antithesis is not between Moses and Paul but between Moses and Christ. Christ is the source of the power and the confidence of the apostle; he is the undimmed brightness which was announced and prefigured by the fading brightness of the countenance of Moses.

Paul has created a theological problem in 3:18 by the identification of the Lord with the Spirit, whether the Lord means the Father (as the context suggests) or the Son (its usual meaning in Paul). The passage cannot be understood in a Trinitarian sense. The Spirit is both that spirit which is opposed to the letter of the law (3:6) and that freedom which is opposed to the slavery of the law. Although Paul uses the word "slavery" in both Galatians and Romans, he does not use it here. However, it is by becoming free from the Law through Christian freedom that the believers "are turned into the image they reflect"; what they reflect is the Spirit of the Lord. When we say that the passage is not Trinitarian we do not mean that Paul was as conscious as we are of the rigorous use of Trinitarian terms; he allowed himself a freedom of the use of the terms which the modern theologian is unable to share.

In speaking of the trials and hopes of the apostolate (4:7—5:10) Paul returns to the theme of his own sufferings in the apostolic mission. The recurrence of this theme in II Cor shows how deeply Paul was wounded by the dispute with the Corinthians; and the very candor of his confession saves him from the charge of self-pity. His sufferings—which include his failures—remind him of his weakness; he is a cheap earthenware vessel in which treasure is stored. His power is not his own but the power of Christ, without which he could not sustain the daily death which the apostolate requires. In the person of Paul, the death and the life of Jesus are revealed.

The thought of the death and the life of Jesus brings Paul to think of his own mortality and of the decay which precedes it. Whether from failure and fatigue or from a bout with illness, Paul shows an awareness that his vital powers are limited and some day will fail. The earthenware vessel will break. But he who dies with Jesus rises to eternal life; and in this assurance he finds the strength to sustain himself in the daily death of the apostolic mission. As Paul says in other epistles, the risen life has already begun in baptism, and earthly life is an exile from the Lord with whom the risen is united when he is released from his "tent." There is a brief allusion to the homeless wandering of the nomad which is contrasted with the permanent residence of the city dweller. Ultimately, then, the apostle sees the difference between life and death as unimportant; what is important is being present to the Lord, whether it is by faith, as now, or by actual sight, in the risen life.

When Paul turns to the apostolate in action (5:11—6:13) he again responds indirectly to his critics, who seem to have charged him with acting unreasonably. The new life for all men which the death of Christ has opened is enough to make a man slightly unreasonable. The love for Christ which "overwhelms" Paul is enough to make him slightly unreasonable. In I Cor 1:25 Paul had said that the foolishness of God is wiser than human wisdom. If this is the case, Paul does not feel insulted if he is charged with acting unreasonably.

This makes Paul firm in his determination not to accept the values of the "flesh"—the principle of physical and moral weakness. His rejection of the knowledge of Christ "in the flesh" is obscurely put. Possibly some of his adversaries had said that he was not a genuine apostle because he had not known Jesus personally. Paul asserts elsewhere that he had seen the risen Jesus; but this could hardly be knowledge "in the flesh." Knowledge of Jesus in the flesh could refer to the expectation of the secular Messiah (mentioned in the Gospels as shared by the disciples). If Paul himself shared the same expectation, only this passage suggests it. But Paul is cutting loose from his Jewish past. In Christ there is a new creation, meaning in the biblical sense that a new world and a new humanity are produced. That Christ is the new Adam who begins a new race is a theme of Romans.

The only reference to the past in this new creation is reconciliation; for man is not made from clay but exists in a state of sin and death. Jesus' identity with man has made him sin, although he is sinless; man is a sinner by definition. The apostles are ambassadors, ministers of reconciliation, bringing terms of peace in the same way that ambassadors bring terms of peace between warring nations.

The authentic commission of these ambassadors is proved by their suffering; this theme recurs. The ambassadors of that reconciliation which was achieved through the cross can prove their authenticity only by sharing the cross. Chaper 11 below resumes this theme, and there the contrast between Paul who suffers and the "arch-apostles" who do not is explicit. Here it is implicit, and this suggests that the latter chapters were dictated at a different time, even if it is not certain that they form a different letter.

Paul suddenly becomes aware that his writing has been intensely personal and also quite revealing. He does not apologize. On the contrary, he asks that the Corinthians will deal with him on an equally personal basis and with a similar lack of constraint. Their relationship is a relationship of love and not of official structure. One realizes that most modern church officers could not appeal to such a relationship and be believed.

The warning against communication with unbelievers (6:13—7:1), as we have noticed, is regarded by many interpreters as a fragment foreign to the context; chapter 7, verse 2 easily follows immediately upon 6:13a. The admonition against bad associations is related to none of the problems of Corinth, either in this context or elsewhere in the letters. It is a far more rigorous statement concerning association with unbelievers than I Cor 5:9-10, where it is recognized that total separation from the world is impossible. This passage refers expressly to unbelievers and cannot be interpreted to mean avoidance of sinners among members of the church. Either Paul's thought on the topic changed radically or he is not the author of this passage. The passage does, however, use the theme of the believer as the temple of God, which is certainly a theme of Paul (I Cor 3:16; 6:19). But the application of this theme to fornication, which is certainly sinful (6:19), is not parallel to the admonition, which warns not against sharing sin but against sharing any activity, presumably even innocent activity. The passage must remain doubtfully Pauline.

As we have mentioned, 7:2 immediately follows 6:13a. The highly personal tone of the correspondence is maintained, whereas this tone is missing in the intervening verses. After all he has said about his pain, Paul affirms that this has in no way altered his feelings toward the Corinthians, and he hopes that it has not altered theirs. He now relives in narrative this recent experience. He remained in Macedonia without repose, upset both by the "quarrels" involved in the apostolic mission and by his anxiety about his relations with Corinth. Then Titus arrived, a messenger of joy, and Paul's gloom was dispelled.

Now his thoughts turn from the sufferings of the apostle to the sufferings of those whom the apostle had to admonish.

Their change of heart seems to attest that he had caused them pain; he had written and spoken sharply, and the infliction of pain was deliberate. It also involved a risk. Now that the effort has been successful Paul feels no need to apologize for the pain he inflicted. It is suffering "in God's way," and this suffering is redemptive. It seems that Paul runs another risk in saying that the pain he caused the Corinthians was good for them but his plea is so ingenuous that no one could take offense. And after all that was said in the early portion of the letter (and what is said in chapters 10-13 following), it is almost inconsistent for Paul to say that the Corinthians have shown themselves in every way blameless in this affair. If they are blameless, is he delicately and implicitly saying that the fault is all his?

Perhaps his statement of complete confidence in them and his readiness to catch any loose blame that is floating around has something to do with what follows. We have seen that some interpreters wonder whether these chapters belong with this epistle. As the letter is composed, it shows awareness of the fact that one does not scold others just before he is going to ask them for a large favor which cannot be done without some sacrifice. No explanation is necessary to show why Paul might have postponed the begging to another letter after the scolding and the reconciliation were past. But Paul was ingenuous in dealing with people. If he was urging that they do the right thing in dealing with their apostle and in contributing to the poor in Jerusalem, he saw no reason why the two requests should not be made in the same letter.

Chapter 8-9 are a plea for a collection to be taken up for the poor of the Palestinian church. The occasion of this collection is not clearly known. We have suggested that besides a famine, the Palestinian church, surrounded by a Jewish community, may have been submitted to economic harassment. Paul's interest in the collection was, of course, motivated by charity in the best sense of the word; but he saw as well that this service would help to unify the Jewish and Gentile Christians. Employing a rather common rhetorical device Paul opens by speaking of the generosity of the

Macedonian churches (Thessalonica, Philippi, Beroea). Like the Corinthians, there were not many wealthy among them; to give anything was to give more than they could afford. The offering of their own selves refers to those who joined Paul's missionary groups.

In this case Paul is not above flattery. The Corinthians, he says, are generously endowed—not with wealth, but with the virtues which will enable them to be generous. Jesus is proposed as an example; this example has a special interest apart from the collection, for it is the earliest statement in the New Testament of the pre-existent Christ. The incarnation was the original "share-the-wealth" plan, but it was a real impoverishment of Jesus; the theme is the same as the "emptying of self" of Philippians 2:6-7. Paul does not suggest such an impoverishment for the Corinthians; one is not asked to do what Paul has just said Jesus did, to enrich others by impoverishing himself. Almost casually he proposes a principle of charitable giving which has never been improved: We should strive neither to enrich others nor to impoverish ourselves (Francis of Assisi is not for everyone), but we should strive for equality—at least to reduce the great difference between those who have and those who have not. Paul fortifies this by a midrashic quotation about the manna, a gift of God which it was impossible to hoard.

Paul recommends the committee who will take up the collection: Titus, his own representative, and two others who are unnamed. These two are appointed by the churches, and there is more here than meets the eye; they are auditors. Paul himself abstains from any actual handling of the money; it is thought that 12:16-18 imply that malfeasance of funds was one of the charges laid against Paul.

The opening verse of chapter 9 is a strange sentence to follow 8:24; yet it is addressed to "Achaia," which must mean Corinth. Paul admits to having used the same tactics of fostering rivalry in Macedonia; but he confesses an exaggeration in saying that Achaia has been ready for a year. Now they must take care not to make him a liar.

Another theological argument for almsgiving is employed—the argument that God withholds his blessings from the ungenerous. To this is added the same plea used in the Sermon on the Mount, that one must trust in God to supply the needs of those who share their goods with the more needy. In addition, the generous giver reflects credit on the God in whom he believes; he is the agent of God's goodness, and makes it easier for the unbeliever to come to faith.

Whether these two chapters are doublets or not, they represent Paul's approach to fund raising, which has been one of the major activities of the church since Paul's time. Rarely if ever have contributions been sought with such a solid theological motivation. If the church is going to continue to solicit contributions, those who solicit and those who give ought to study these chapters.

We have mentioned the doubts concerning chapters 10-13 and the place of these chapters in the epistle. The change of tone is evident from a cursory reading. Paul responds to adversaries not mentioned elsewhere; they seem to be persons of some importance. The fact that Paul calls them "arch-apostles" and "counterfeit apostles" suggests that they had the title of apostle rather than the opposite. They appear to be Judaizers, of the type mentioned in Galatians. He treats once more of the apostolate, and directly of his personal apostolate; he defends himself. We are in no position here to resolve the question whether the passage belongs to I Cor or not.

Paul first replies to a charge of weakness (10:1-11). His adversaries say that he writes strong letters, but that he has no presence and is no speaker. Paul's first response is to state in another way what he has said in earlier discussions of the apostolate; the power of the apostolate is not the personal power of each apostle but the power of the gospel—the power of God—of which he is the vessel. Paul does not often appeal to his authority, but he does so here because of the implication that personal weakness makes him an ineffective apostle. This is contrary to Paul's whole idea of the apostolate. Nevertheless, since the adversary seems to speak without personal acquaintance with Paul, he assures his readers that he is the man who appears in his letters.

Paul is charged with boasting (10:12-18); it is difficult to make the charge more specific than this on the basis of Paul's reply. In fact, he answers only that it has no reference to the Corinthians. He is the apostle of Corinth and needs no boast; it is the same kind of compliment which he has given earlier in the epistles. He is not claiming credit for work done by others, nor is he comparing his achievement with the achievements of others. It appears that his adversaries were making such claims. The apostle should not write his own recommendations; if he does the work of God, God will recommend him.

Self-defense compels Paul to engage in self-praise. He does this with distaste and with profuse apologies. He explains that he has the jealousy of a matchmaker—a feeling which the modern reader finds hard to understand. There is a danger that the bride will be seduced from Christ her spouse; the danger has not yet happened. Actually this is the most severe rebuke uttered up to this point in I-II Cor. And the sarcasm with which he describes the Corinthians' readiness to hear a new gospel about a new Jesus conferring a new spirit is extremely harsh. Here Paul sounds like the Paul of Galatians, where he said that even an angel of God who proclaimed a different gospel should be rejected (Gal. 1:8). He does not say here what the new gospel is; we observe that he speaks of the "arch-apostles" with more reserve than he shows in Galatians.

The charge to which Paul replies in 11:7-15 is not specified. It seems that the "arch-apostle" found fault with him for accepting no fee for his ministry. Paul again becomes sarcastic, as well he might; to be criticized for rejecting personal gain, even gain which could be accepted without fault, is enough to arouse resentment in the most patient of men. Paul ironically says that he robbed other churches for the sake of the Corinthians. That Paul accepted support from the Macedonians for his mission in Corinth is not in harmony with his profession of independence in I Cor 9, but it is not in flat contradiction. What the Macedonians gave him was not a fee for the ministry in Macedonia, but an outright gift, a contribution to the ministry not in Macedonia but elsewhere. Paul felt he could accept such a gift without violating his principle of self-support; even Paul had problems concerning contributions. But with the problems he knows that his adversaries make no effort at all to spare the churches contributions for their own support. This is enough for them to be labeled "counterfeit apostles"; Paul compares them to Satan disguised as an angel. We do not know what they said about Paul, but we wonder whether any reconciliation was ever made after this exchange.

Paul feels it necessary to interrupt his defense with another apology for making it (11:16-21). He thinks that such defense is foolishness, but this thought affords another occasion for sarcasm. He can be foolish with the Corinthians, who suffer fools gladly, even the fools who impose on them (11:20); these can be no other than the counterfeit apostles. Paul is ashamed of being a weak fool, but not a bullying fool.

How shall Paul attest the authenticity of his apostolate? First he affirms his Jewishness. It is fairly clear that at this point in his career Paul has become the great renegade, not only to Jews but to Jewish Christians. Nevertheless, the fascination which the mother race and the mother church exercised was a fact of life. Paul regarded it as unimportant, but for those who thought Jewishness marked the true aristocrats of the church Paul could claim purity of blood. He does not appeal to the call of Jesus; rather, he appeals to suffering, which he proposes as the true test of the apostolate. There is no reason to doubt his claim that he labored and suffered more than any other. The recital is quite circumstantial. The concession of personal involvement with the churches and the believers (11:28-29) is touching. One is persuaded that this recital of the pains and perils of the mission does not suggest that persecution was a normal part of the life of the apostolic church. It is in character with the rest of Paul's self-defense to suppose that this too is not free from sarcasm; he means to imply that the "arch-apostles" exercise a mission which is free from pain and peril, and even from discomfort. For some reason Paul remembers with particular clarity his undignified escape from Damascus, perhaps because this was the occasion on which he recognized he was nearest to death.

The apostle must have a special communication from God; he is the successor of the Israelite prophets, who spoke the word of God. Paul's mystical experiences (12:1-7) suggest the apocalyptic writings of Judaism rather than the prophetic books of the Old Testament. He describes what in modern mystical theology is called rapture; the ambiguity he felt as to whether he remained in his body was an experience which later mystics attested for themselves.

Paul's experience was ineffable in the strict sense of the term and, therefore, he refuses to attempt to describe it. Other mystics also have said that the height of the mystical experience lies beyond language. But this experience was not "revelation" as the gospel is revelation. It cannot be formulated even in the extremely simple creed of the primitive church.

Furthermore, Paul has no commission to share this experience with others, and, indeed, as he tells it there is nothing he could share. He could promise the faithful nothing more than a prospect that they might have a similar experience. It does not seem to be an apostolic experience. If this is directed at the adversaries, then they must have claimed such visions and revelations; by definition, an attitude such as this makes them early Gnostics, for they believed that the gospel must be enriched through revelations made to elect souls. Paul's language, while it is harsh enough when he speaks of "another gospel," does not suggest that the arch-apostles manifested the excesses which the church, from the second century onward, had to combat and reject.

Aware of the danger of pride in mystical experience, Paul is grateful for the thorn in the flesh, the angel of Satan who brought him pain. His commentators have been unable to discern the nature of the affliction. The most probable as well as the most common interpretation is that some relatively permanent physical affliction is meant (rather than concupiscence, which afflicts everyone, or persecution, about which Paul has just boasted). It must have been an affliction which hampered his mission. This explains both Paul's prayer for deliverance and the answer: God's grace supplies all needed power, and is most manifested in weakness.

Apparently the authenticity of the apostle was expected to be assured by signs and wonders (12:11-13). This, like the charismatic gifts of the primitive church, introduces the modern stranger to a world of thought in which he feels himself a stranger. Paul is on the way to saying that the greatest miracle of the church is genuine love, as it is the greatest charism (I Cor 13). But in the world of the first century—Jewish and pagan, as well as Christian—wonderful works were expected and they happened. Paul allows no inferiority in this respect; the arch-apostles have performed no wonders which he has not performed himself. He has deprived the Corinthians of nothing except charges for his ministry—a final sarcasm on the charge that he has made personal gain. This charge must have been so obviously false that it took the form seen in 12:16-18; indeed Paul did not demand fees, but he tricked the Corinthians into giving him money. The refutation of this is simply a reference to Titus and his companion; they must have been men with such a reputation for integrity that no more was needed than their approval. Since this appears to refer to the collection of chapters 8-9, we are again involved in the question of the unity of the letter. It is scarcely possible, even if Paul did ramble, that in the same letter he should announce the coming of a collector and auditors and respond to the charge that the collection was a device for self-enrichment.

Paul concludes his defense by saying that it is addressed to God rather than to the Corinthians (12:19). This implies that the charges moved Paul to a serious examination of himself and his conduct. He satisfies his own conscience. Now he is afraid that he may find the Corinthians falling into new vices and unrepentant of the old ones. This attitude is hard to reconcile with the statement of confidence with which chapter 7 concluded. Likewise the reference to an intended visit (his third) is difficult to reconcile with the two visits which were followed by the visit of Titus and the reconciliation. The admonitions which follow do not indicate that the reconciliation which preceded chapters 1-7 has occurred. If it had, then something happened between the writing of chapters 7 and 10-13 which threw the whole problem open again. No explanation of the problem is entirely satisfactory. But the theological and spiritual value of the letter does not depend on the biography of Paul; this is fortunate, because we do not have a biography of Paul. In 13:5-10 Paul faces the common problems of the apostle and the teacher: Is it the growth of the disciples or personal success which concerns him most? Like so many, Paul probably found that there is no completely reassuring answer to this question; for to ask the question is to make an answer impossible.

The conclusion, it is evident, may not have followed what now stands before it. It is of special interest; it is the first Trinitarian formula of such clarity in the New Testament.

Chater Six

EPISTLE TO THE ROMANS

Scholars generally place the composition of Romans in Corinth in the winter of 57-58. According to the Acts of the Apostles, Paul's plans to visit Rome (see 15:22-23 below) did not materialize; his journey to Rome was delayed by his arrest in Jerusalem, and he finally reached Rome as a prisoner whose case was appealed to the imperial tribunal (Acts 21-28). Paul does not make it clear why he wished to visit Rome, and why he wrote his own introduction. He does not mention Peter (Cephas) by name since he probably had not yet reached Rome.

We do not know that the community was large and influential; and the letter itself leaves the question open as to whether the church was predominantly Jewish, predominantly Gentile, or a balanced mixture of the two. That Paul chose to visit Rome and write his own letter of introduction suggests that the Roman church early attained an eminence in numbers and position; and primitive Christianity was much more an urban movement than a rural movement. Rome would attract the movement; the largest city the world had yet known, it was a "world city" as no other city had been. Possibly Paul, a known controversial figure, judged it wise to introduce himself by setting forth a summary of his doctrine about salvation through Christ and the relations of Christians to the Law; for these are the points treated at length in the letter. As we shall see below, there are reasons for thinking that several churches received a copy of this letter; the letter is best understood as a defense of the orthodoxy of Paul's teaching.

The address is unusually long (1:1-8). It summarizes the

gospel ("the Good News") as the news about Jesus Christ, through whom Paul has received the mission to preach the obedience of faith to all nations—which seems to suggest a Gentile audience. The Christology of 1:3-4 is of the type called "primitive." Paul distinguishes between the "historical" Jesus (according to the flesh), the son of David, and the "proclaimed" or "revealed" Son of God, whose power and full reality were first disclosed in his resurrection. The thanksgiving (1:8-15) is also unusually long; Paul has to apologize for writing the Romans and for wishing to visit them. It is almost a slip when he declares his desire to "bring the Good News" to them; he is not their apostle.

Paul begins the announcement of the Good News with the description of the need for the Good News. The need is first shown in the pagan (or Greek) world (1:16-32); for Paul, Jews and Greeks comprise all of humanity. Paul begins his exposition by the use of the two key words of the epistle, righteousness (JB "justice") and faith. Most English versions prefer the translation "righteousness" (with the Authorized Version) to the JB's "justice"; the word "righteousness" has the advantage of no extrabiblical usage and therefore of being nearly meaningless to most readers. "Justice" in English suggests the processes of law, and these are not the processes of redemption and forgiveness; we have no processes of "justice" which deliver the guilty from punishment. Where we would speak of justice Paul speaks of "anger" (1:18). The Hebrew word which "righteousness" reflects is a saving attribute; and God, when he deals "righteously" with humanity, does not merely punish men for their sins but delivers them from their sins. God alone can display "righteousness" of this kind. There is nothing man can do to make himself the object of this saving righteousness, not even the observance of the Law which God has revealed.

Pagans, surprisingly enough, are not excused by ignorance. Paul seems to be thinking not of the ordinary man but of the intellectuals of the Hellenistic-Roman world; Paul was aware of philosophy and learning, although as a Pharisee he probably refused to learn anything from it (see I Corinthians

1:18—2:16). Paul's rebuke is directed against those who wickedly imprison the truth (1:18), and this can hardly mean the poor and the uneducated. We do not know why Paul may have thought that the Roman church was more influenced by learning than his own churches. Jewish contempt for Greek learning was matched by Greek contempt for Jewish rites, which educated men regarded as superstition.

In this invective against pagan vices Paul reflects his pharisaic background. He affirms that the world itself is evidence of the existence of God—by which he means the one and only true God who has revealed himself to the Jews. The implication of this argument can only be that educated pagans did recognize the one true God in the God in whom the Jews believed. Instead of admitting this, Paul charges, they have concealed the truth about God. This dishonesty has made it impossible for them to maintain even basic moral standards, and he sums up the whole structure of Hellenistic-Roman civilization as morally corrupt. His rabbinical background appears in his harshness toward homosexuality; this has to be called a characteristic vice of Greek and Roman antiquity, praised by philosophers and poets. The best known of the philosophers is Plato. The best known of the poets is Sappho of Lesbos, whose home gave its name to the love of which she sang. Jewish teaching abominated the vice which in the Bible is associated with the name of Sodom.

Paul's condemnation of the moral quality of Hellenistic-Roman culture is supported by the history and literature of the period, although Paul does not attend to certain redeeming features, such as the philosophy of Stoicism. The Stoics maintained a relatively high level of morality based on reason. Stoicism was not a widely popular philosophy, but then no rigorous system of ethics has ever been widely popular. The Roman world was vast and complex, and general moral judgments about its people are probably no more and no less valid than they are about our own contemporary world. From certain points of view one could apply Paul's lines word for word to contemporary Europe and

America. Many would accept them as valid, even though they do not apply in their fullness to millions of people.

The question of the natural knowledge of God which Paul has opened up has been pursued, especially in recent times, in apologetics and philosophy. As I have restated Paul's proposition—a restatement which attempts to reflect the thinking of a Christian rabbi—it is not the same as most apologetic thinking; Paul was not concerned with "some idea" of a supreme being, but with the God of Abraham, Isaac, Jacob and Moses. It appears that in these terms he overstates his case. The leading thinkers of the Greek and Roman world were no more guilty of idolatry than Paul was. On the other hand, Paul's remarks about the Law in the chapters that follow do not leave much room for the apologetic presentation of the Law to pagans; yet the God of the fathers had revealed himself in the Law. Paul's intention in this passage is simply to show that the Gentiles stand in need of the Good News to deliver them from unbelief and moral corruption. The point is valid, if overstated.

The Jews would agree enthusiastically with Paul's strictures on Hellenistic morals. Paul suddenly turns to them (2:1—3:20), although he does not use the word "Jew" immediately. The Jews as a group were not guilty of the gross sins of the flesh of which Paul accuses the pagans. He first accuses the Jews of unrepentance, a strangely vague fault, and the English word is perhaps misleading; rather, he means self-righteousness, the refusal to see any fault in themselves. Here Paul passes the same judgment which Jesus in the Gospels passes upon the Pharisees: Avoiding the crass sins of sensuality, they fall into the vices of pride and cruelty. These are almost the occupational vices of "religious" persons.

The pride of the Jews was their Law, the revealed will of God, which imposed a much more rigorous morality than any pagan moral system. Paul, not entirely consistent with his rhetoric in chapter 1, states that the pagan who observes the obligations of the Law is just as good as the Jew who observes it and better than the Jew who does not observe it. This passage is incorrectly adduced to show that Paul believed in "the natural law" or "the law of reason." These are Stoic phrases which Paul could have known; he may allude to them in 2:14. Paul never uses the Greek word for "law" without reference, explicit or implicit, to the only true law, the law which God revealed to Moses. Conscience, that moral judgment of reason which every man possesses to some degree, will distinguish between right and wrong, and thus show that the "Law" is written on the heart of the Gentiles, as it was written on tablets of stone for the Jews. And conscience does for the Gentiles what the Law does for the Jews. The phrase may echo Jeremiah 31:31-34, but if it does it is used in a sense which differs from the meaning of the phrase in Jeremiah.

Since Paul denies that the Law of Moses is a means of salvation, he never meant to say that the natural law of reason is a means of salvation; he meant that the reasonable pagan can observe the Law (and he can hardly mean the ceremonial law). Both the pagan and the Jew, whether they live by the Law of Moses or the law of nature and reason, are in need of redemption. Paul is even less respectful toward circumcision in their literature. Paul does not join them in jest here (although he came close to it in Galatians 5:12); but (borrowing from Jeremiah 9:24-26) he affirms that the only true circumcision is circumcision of the heart. His remarks about the Law and about circumcision seem almost deliberately calculated to irritate Jews.

When Paul speaks about Jews he finds it difficult to be consistent. He asks himself whether the Jew has an advantage over the Gentile and answers in the affirmative; the Jew received the revelation of God, and it would seem to approach blasphemy to deny that this is an advantage. But when he has enumerated this "in the first place," there is no second place in the list. Immediately he faces the problem of Jewish infidelity, and he declares that God's fidelity does not depend on human fidelity. Then in 3:9 he is compelled to contradict what he had said in 3:2; the Jew has no advantage, since the privilege of the revelation has in a certain sense been negated by Jewish infidelity to the revelation. All men alike lie under the dominion of sin; and this thesis is supported by a chain of texts from Scripture. The universal dominion of sin exists despite the Law, and Paul here prepares the way for his discussion of the Law in chapter 7. He is satisfied with the point that no one is made righteous by keeping the Law, because Jews have not kept the Law. The Law merely points out what is wrong; it furnishes no help to its own observance.

Paul is not as specific in accusing the Jews of sin as he is in accusing the Gentiles, and with good reason; all our information is that Jewish morality in general was much more rigorous both in its principles and in its practices than the morality of the Hellenistic-Roman world. The charge of theft and adultery (2:21-22) is so general that it is fairly safe to make; it is also fairly meaningless. But what Paul meant by temple robbery *(ibid.)* has bewildered his commentators since the first commentators (the JB does not even attempt to comment on this verse). This crime (Greek *hierosylia*) was regarded from early Greek times as the peak of impiety; and Paul very probably wrote this under the influence of Greek ideas. If Paul had known the Gospels he could have drawn from such passages as Matthew 23. He does not, and in fact is ultimately less severe to the Jews than the Synoptic Gospels, and presumably less severe than Jesus himself.

There is no deliverance from sin either for Jew or for Greek except through the righteousness (JB "justice") of God, first revealed in the Law and the Prophets and now in Jesus Christ (3:21-31). There is no hope except through Christ. The JB says that Christ was appointed to sacrifice his life (3:25). This paraphrase conceals the reference to the "throne of mercy" or "mercy seat" (Exodus 25:19), a metal plate on the top of the ark of the covenant before which rites of propitiation and atonement were performed. Paul as yet avoids saying that Christ himself is the actual "material" of the rite of atonement; rather, Christ's presence makes the ritual atonement effective. Naturally Paul means that the atonement performed "before" Christ is far more effective than the atonement performed before the ark. Here he is using the language figuratively, not exactly.

Paul's thesis excludes Jewish "boasting"; and it must be conceded that "boastful" has often described the attitude of the Jews toward the Gentiles. Boasting is excluded by the "law"; and by a striking paradox Paul means by this "the law of faith." As Paul uses the two terms, one excludes the other; but he is not anxious to exclude the Jews from faith. Faith alone makes one righteous, whether it is achieved with the Law or without the Law.

Paul is moved to this position by the thought that there is only one God, a truth which Judaism held as the most sacred of all beliefs. Once this truth is professed, it follows of necessity that he is the God of the Gentiles; for it was intolerable, even in Judaism, that God had no providence except for the Jews. Paul saw that the Jews' claim of privilege ultimately denied the providence of God for the Gentiles. There could be no "chosen people" unless it included all of mankind. Paul denies that this idea is a rejection of the Law; rather, it is an affirmation of the Law. But his dispute with the Jews was precisely this: He claimed that the Law had no meaning unless it was fulfilled in Christ.

Man achieves righteousness only by faith; and this is illustrated by the example of Abraham. This example, used in Galatians 3:6-18, is worked out at greater length here (4:1-25). Paul's argument is based on a verse from Genesis (15:6) and the arrangement of the material in Genesis 12-25, the story of Abraham. The verse from Genesis furnishes one of Paul's key ideas, faith and righteousness. Loosely paraphrased, the verse means that Abraham believed that God would keep his promise, and this was counted to Abraham's credit. Obviously these two words did not have the theological weight in Genesis which they have in the writings of Paul, and still less, the weight which they have received in later theological language. In this instance, Paul's use of the biblical text is, like so much of his use of the Bible, strictly rabbinical; the words of the text are given all the weight they can bear, for God speaks to all men and all times through the Bible. Through the faith and righteousness of Abraham, God reveals by anticipation the saving faith and righteousness which he reveals fully in Christ Jesus. Faith in Christ is belief that righteousness is created only by God through Christ and with no human effort, not even by observing the Law. If the reader finds that Paul's argument appears repetitious, his impression is correct. The positive consequences of faith (such as the commandment of love) are developed later.

The promise which Abraham believes occurs in Genesis 15 and the circumcision occurs in Genesis 17. From this arrangement Paul argues that faith and righteousness preceded circumcision; at the time he became righteous, Abraham was a Gentile made righteous by faith, although Paul avoids this offensive statement. Furthermore, those who are circumcised without faith do not receive righteousness. Thus, Abraham is truly the father of all believers for the Gentiles, but not for the unbelieving Jews. Paul attacks Jewish pride in Abraham as it is attacked in Matthew 3:9; Luke 3:8; John 8:33-40.

On the same principle of chronology Abraham did not, of course, observe the Law; it had not yet been revealed. Some rabbis, almost as if anticipating Paul's argument, asserted that the Law was created before the world (and consequently is not enumerated among the works of the Six Days). Again on the principle of chronology, the promise that Abraham would inherit the world was made before circumcision and the Law (4:13). This promise is not found in the biblical text; it was a rabbinical interpretation of the promise that Abraham would have a progeny too numerous to count. Paul uses this rabbinical interpretation for his own purpose; he sees the fulfillment of the promise in the faith of the Gentiles, which was not the intention of the rabbis.

The JB has smoothed out the Old English (and Latin) paradoxical version of 4:18, "In hope he believed against hope." Old age and sterility forbade the hope of children to Abraham and Sarah except in the power of him who brings the dead to life and calls the nonexistent into being. By the strength of such faith the Christian believes in the resurrection of Christ, the conversion of the Gentiles and the resurrection of all to life everlasting.

With chapter 5 Paul begins his exposition of what salvation means (see headline in JB). He introduces this statement (5:1-11) by bringing together all of the key words in the epistle. The righteousness, which is the work of God responding to faith, brings peace with God (5:1) and reconciliation (5:10-11). The "state of grace" (5:2) thus achieved is not the "state of grace" of which the modern Catholic speaks; it is the enjoyment of God's favor, synonymous with peace and reconciliation. It is an assurance of a future share in the glory of God (5:2).

Paul now introduces a theme to which he will return in this and later letters. Suffering becomes a means of growth in hope and in love. We are redeemed by the suffering and death of Christ; the value of his suffering is communicated to that of the believer. We would not think of suffering as generating hope, but Paul does. In suffering one is more aware of the gift of the Holy Spirit, the gift of God's love for us. The love of God in 5:5 is ambiguous, for it could mean either God's love for us or our love of God. Interpreters are mostly agreed that the context demands a reference to the love of God for us. The reference to the death of Christ brings Paul to a somewhat digressive reflection on the unworthiness of mankind for whom Christ died. In the preceding chapters he has been at pains to show how both Jews and Greeks need redemption. Now it strikes him with a novel force how unlovely, ungracious and revolting men are—their desirable qualities come from the gift of God in Christ.

Romans 5:12-21 is the most famous and the most discussed passage of the epistles of Paul, indeed of the entire Bible. On this passage alone are based the entire doctrine and theology of original sin. These important dogmatic developments occurred during controversies with the Pelagians (in which Augustine led in developing the Catholic position) in the fifth and sixth centuries, and the Council of Trent in the sixteenth century, during which the Catholic position was further developed in controversy with the Lutherans. Catholics easily read Paul in the light of the development of doctrine; it is important to remember that most of this development is not in the text of Paul, but represents conclusions derived from a great deal of extremely complicated theological thinking.

The purpose of the passage is to show the superabundance of the saving act of Christ; to illustrate this Paul draws a parallel between one man, Adam, and another man, Christ. The parallel is not intended to be perfect. Great as the damage wrought by one man was, the salvation exceeds the damage at every point. The damage is the admission into the world of sin and death; this duet occupies Paul's attention through chapters 6-8. Paul confuses his argument and his readers by digressing from the thesis on 5:13-14. An imaginary objection is solved, the objection that before the Law there was no "sin" in the proper sense of the word. This imaginary objection did not trouble Paul in 1:16-32, and it is not clear why it troubles him here. He dismisses it by pointing out the universality of death, and thus assumes without explicit argument that death is a penalty of sin in every human being. Genesis 2:17 and 3:19 would furnish him sufficient evidence. The antithesis between Adam and Christ is drawn out through a series of nearly synonymous statements, culminating in the gift of eternal life through righteousness.

Paul does not clearly say that the universal sin of man is hereditary, and it is not certain that this was on his mind. The doctrine has grown from that which is better known, the saving work of Christ; Paul is emphatic that this is a gift, unearned, impossible to human effort. Doctrinal development has extended the same principle of gratuity to the relation of men with the first sinner, and inherited guilt is a logical conclusion. The doctrine was developed in response to Pelagius, who taught that both Adam and Christ influenced men by their example. If each man is his own Adam, then each man would be his own Christ—a conclusion which Pelagius did not draw. What Paul wished to state almost repeats what he said in chapters 1-3, that the dominion of sin is universal and inescapable.

In 6:1, perhaps frightened by his own eloquence, Paul asks whether, in view of the fact that man is helpless and God is all-powerful, it might be simpler to renounce any struggle against sin and let God do his work. Paul answers by a statement of the relation of the Christian with Christ which is somewhat new in the epistles and of great importance in the development of Christian doctrine. The experience of salvation is a re-enactment in the Christian of the saving act of Christ. This experience is effectively symbolized by the rite of baptism, "effectively" here meaning that the rite effects the reality which it symbolizes. In baptism the Christian dies with Christ and rises with Christ to a new life, life eternal. Physical death terminates physical life; for the Christian, sacramental death terminates sin. As the rising Christ can die no more, so the rising Christian can sin no more. He is dead to sin.

Plainly this raises questions, but Paul does not deal with them here. The Christian must make a personal decision not to sin. Paul's point is that he can make it, and it is inconceivable that one who can make this decision will refuse it. Paul has not yet learned that one should not easily think that anything is inconceivable. The Christian is no longer a slave to sin, the servitude described in the preceding chapters. As interpreters suggest, Paul may be influenced by the rabbinical theory of adult circumcision. In Jewish law the adult proselyte died; this meant release from all obligations, including marriage and debt. Paul certainly thinks of baptism in these terms, and here of the manumission by death from the slavery of sin. The JB correctly puts "slaves" of righteousness (6:18) in quotation marks. Baptism is not the exchange of one master for another, but of slavery for freedom. It is as irrational for one risen to a new life to choose sin as it would be to choose death.

In 6:15 Paul asks a question which has been asked many times in the history of Christianity. Certainly Paul's insistence on the abolition of the Law, on the supreme power of God and on the freedom conferred by Christ furnished an occasion for some to say that Christian freedom meant that man now rises above the law and above all morality. Since man cannot overcome sin—indeed, man is a slave to sin according to Paul's teaching—freedom means release from the struggle against the impossible, not a mandate to renew it. This bizarre but not unattractive interpretation of the gospel was popular among many of the Gnostic sects of the early centuries; they combined Pauline freedom thus understood with the Gnostic principle that since the body was sin in any case, it did not make much difference what you did with it. The question of Paul suggests that some form of this aberration appeared very early and it seems fairly sure that the sins for which freedom was desired were sexual acts. We have commented in connection with other epistles what a radical departure Christian morality was from the conventional sexual liberty of the Hellenistic-Roman world.

Paul draws a contrast between the "wage" of sin and the present given by God; one is death, the other is eternal life. "Wage" is strictly "rations," the portion of food given to the Roman soldier each day; and so Paul signifies sin as a daily deposit of death, so to speak. This is not the threat of sudden or premature death, but the denial of eternal life. Paul also contrasts the "rations," the minimum portion which is laborious acquired by the slaves of sin, with the gift bestowed without stint or measure. As we have noticed, Paul uses "slavery" figuratively to mean the service of God; but he means that Sin is an exacting, tyrannical and stingy master.

Paul's words about freedom from the Law carry implications which create problems. He approaches these problems by a restatement of the freedom from the Law which comes with baptism, and he again uses the analogy of death. Here it is the death of the husband which frees the wife. Obviously the analogy should not be pressed too far, and Paul comes close to doing this. He almost forgets that in his own belief the one who gave the Law was the Father of our Lord Jesus Christ, who is the new spouse in his figure of the wedding (7:1-6).

But Paul has not entirely forgotten that for Jews the Law is sacred, just and good (7:12). Paul does not wish to say or even to imply that the Law is sin (7:7). Yet he has been at pains to show that the Jews are no better off than the Gentiles in the war against sin, and this in spite of the revelation they have received from God. He faces his own implication that God has been a failure; that God, who alone can overcome sin, has in fact tried to overcome it and has not succeeded. He meets this problem by an appeal to "the other law" within man. In theology, this law has been known as concupiscence; and theological teaching has related concupiscence more closely to the sin of Adam than Paul does in this passage—in fact, the "fall" of man in Christian belief has generally been understood as a "fall" into concupiscence. This is not actually what Paul says here and it shows again that Paul is not nearly as clear on the teaching of "original sin" as the church has been in the development of doctrine.

We referred above to the difference between Jewish and Gentile morality, both in theory and in practice, in the Hellenistic-Roman world. Jews were conscious of this difference; in this passage Paul shows his awareness. According to most commentators, the "I" of the passage is not the autobiographical "I"; Paul is not describing his personal experience. Nor is it the "I" of humanity in general. It can only be the "I" of the Jew who is subject to the Law and therefore subject to a higher morality than the Gentiles knew. Only of the Gentiles could Paul say that without the Law sin is dead (7:8), which is not entirely consistent with what he states in chapter 1.

In fact it is not simply a statement of "the two laws" which Paul proposes. He recognizes that an informed conscience has moral problems which the ignorant conscience does not have. Does the ignorant conscience then do evil? Moral theologians still argue about the solution of particular cases, but only because they are not sure how much ignorance is tolerable in sincere conscience. Paul may have been less tolerant of the invincibly ignorant conscience than we are. His point in this passage is that the informed conscience suffers simply because of its knowledge. But there is another factor which he less clearly recognizes; it is the instinctive or demonic quality in man which leads him to seek out what is forbidden. This is the "law of the members" which fights against the "law of the mind." Paul attributes this law not to the "I," the true self, but to personified Sin; and "Sin" here plays the role which popular Christian belief later attributed to the devil. There is less inconsistency in Paul's personification of Sin, for in his theology Sin is a reality to which man dies in baptism.

By this exposition, Paul saves the Law as a work of God and at the same time maintains his thesis that God has worked effectively against sin only through Jesus Christ. Christ is the only deliverance from this body "doomed to death" (7:24). He has given strength to his earlier assertion that the Law shows what is wrong but furnishes no help to its own observance. Everyone recognizes Paul's description of the interior conflict which is an essential part of the human scene. No one else, not even the rabbis, proposed a way of life in which man could rise above this conflict. What Paul does here is to refuse sin the rights of the city of man. He will not, like the rabbis and the philosophers, take sin for granted as a part of the human scene. God has moved effectively against it through Christ, even against the Sin which each man feels is deeply planted within his own personality. It is not a part of his personality if he has died with Christ to sin and risen with Christ to righteousness. This is Life; Sin is Death.

The Law is effectively annulled; in chapter 8, Paul turns to the problem of a possible vacuum created by the disappearance of the Law. It is replaced by another "law" (the word is again used metaphorically), the law of the spirit of life (8:2), which releases the Christian from all condemnation. In chapter 8, the words "spirit" and "spiritual" suddenly occur with much greater frequency. "Spirit" is opposed to "flesh." As Paul uses "flesh," it is not merely the flesh which in popular devout language has reference to the activities of sex; and spirit is not opposed precisely to this aspect of the "flesh." Flesh is Paul's word for man as a being physically and morally corruptible—mortal and sinful, subject to the anti-God pair of Sin and Death. When man dies and rises in

Christ to a new life, this life is not carnal; it is the life of the Spirit of God, the Spirit of Christ (Paul uses both terms). The contrast between the spiritual and the carnal man will be specified in Paul's treatment of Christian morality. His interest here is to affirm the reality of the principle which enables men to live free of the Law and free of sin; Paul insists that the Spirit, like "life," is within the individual person, i.e. "indwelling."

It does not follow from the indwelling that the believer is an adopted child of God, but Paul makes the point (8:14-17). Commentators remark that there is no adoption in Jewish biblical law, and it is possible that Paul derived the idea from Hellenistic culture. The believer invokes God as Father in the Spirit; Paul had probably never heard of the Lord's prayer. In Paul's terms, this means that prayer to the Father is a charismatic act, like the profession that Jesus is Lord (1 Corinthians 12:3). The sharing of the life of the risen Christ creates the theme of one large family, which is developed in other epistles. The new life in Christ is a heritage, and by loose verbal association Paul reaches the idea of shared sufferings (8:17). The new life does not exclude suffering, although the dominant tone in the writings of Paul is hardly ascetic in the sense that he cultivates suffering for its own sake. But, he does tell his correspondents that their sufferings are inconsiderable in view of the glory which is consummation of the Christian destiny.

By an original turn of thought Paul sees all creation as sharing in both the suffering and the hope of the Christian faith. The theme of the curse of nature (Genesis 3:17-19) as a result of sin is not worked out in the Old Testament. Paul sees creation as frustrated of its purpose (8:20) because man has not attained his purpose. It is, indeed, a common biblical view that creation is understood only as the habitation of man, a view which many of our contemporaries find difficult to sustain. The awaiting of creation for its destiny is likened by Paul to one great birth-pang. The theme is related to the idea of the new heavens and the new earth, found both in the Old Testament (Isaiah 65:17, 66:22) and in the New (2 Peter

3:13, Revelation 21:1); the New Testament passages are derived from the Old Testament.

When the believer, feeling his weakness and the delay of the fulfillment, wishes to address God, he can do so only in the charismatic prayer of the Spirit. Without the Spirit the Christian cannot sustain his hope. When the Spirit speaks in us, God surely hears. In a simple and great profession of faith Paul asserts that God turns all things to good for those who love him. He excludes no one from God's love and does not pretend that a painless world has been achieved.

The closing verses (8:31-39) are often called a hymn by interpreters; the tone is hymnic, even if the form is not. The lines are an expansion of the theme of 8:28, and a rhetorical expression of the assurance which is based on this belief. The union which God has wrought in Christ with the believers cannot be sundered by any power less than God, and Paul enumerates several possible obstacles. Some are known from experience (8:35) and these are more dangerous. Others represent cosmic powers (8:38-39) which were a threat to Paul and his contemporaries. If the modern Christian does not fear them, he will be well to fear the more concrete obstacles of 8:35. Apart from cosmic powers, Paul means that nothing separates the believer from the love of God in Christ Jesus except the personal decision of the believer. As we said above, this is a choice of death rather than life.

In chapters 1-8 Paul has discussed extensively the relations of Christians to the Law. The discussion has more or less compelled him to reach the point which he now takes up —the place of the Jews in God's plan of salvation. Paul was not only a Jew, he was a rabbi; and the reader must remember this personal involvement. His arguments might lead him, as they have led many Christians, simply to dismiss the Jews as of no further importance in the theology of salvation. For Paul, this would be equivalent to charging God with failure—and this would be intolerable. We may add that Paul's treatment should have been the model for all Christian treatments of the problem. It is free of prejudice (Paul could hardly be anti-Semitic!), it is strictly theological and not personal, and he never mentions the share of Jews in Jesus' death.

Paul expresses deep personal feeling, and this should be taken seriously; he even expresses a wish for his own damnation (not permissible in modern moral theology) if this would save his people; Moses is the model for such a wish (Exodus 32:32). Paul enumerates seven privileges of the Jews which follow their election: adoption (rare in the OT, as noticed above; see JB note), the glory (the abiding presence), the covenants, the Law, the cult, the promises (of the Messiah), the patriarchs (men beloved of God). The eighth and greatest privilege, which they have so far refused, is the Messiah—a Jew by nativity. Paul concludes this recital with an ambiguous phrase. Some think that the invocation of God refers to Christ (the JB note argues for this). But this is not Paul's usual style, for whom Christ is the Son of God. Furthermore, it was and is a Jewish practice to utter a doxology when some special act of God is mentioned—in devout modern Judaism, whenever "The Name" is mentioned.

This recital leads to the question whether God has kept his promise. It is not an answer to say that the Jews were unfaithful; Paul has already made the point that the fidelity of God does not depend on the fidelity of man. His actual answer may seem to be an evasion; for he distinguishes between Israel according to the flesh and Israel according to the promise, a distinction he has already made in chapter 4. Even the children of the patriarchs were not all bearers of the promise; God is represented as having to choose between the twins, Esau and Jacob. These are examples of the rabbinical interpretation we have mentioned several times. Paul's point is that God did not choose the Jews because they were a deserving people.

Not satisfied with this answer, Paul then turns to the imagined objection that God is unfair. His answer in one phrase is that since God owes no man anything he cannot be unfair. Evidently, this notion seemed satisfactory to Paul; many of his readers have found that it creates worse problems than those he began with, for much of the theology of predestination historically has leaned on 9:14-24. Only if one thinks of God as Paul thought of him can one speak of God as Paul does in this passage. As a point of fact, most of us, and most of Paul's readers and interpreters, do not think of God as Paul thought of him. God's mercy, as he saw it, is always given, it is never earned. Paul does not imply that God gives and denies it arbitrarily; he does affirm that God need not bestow it in a way which men can always explain. Human standards of justice and mercy do not reach the reality of God; he reaches mercy and justice on a higher level than men can comprehend. If anyone refuses mercy, Paul does not believe God owes him anything. The theologians of predestination have, it seems, attempted to answer precisely the question which Paul said they should not ask. With all this granted, it remains true that Paul's biblical patterns of thought and language remain difficult for the modern reader.

Paul strengthens his statement that God has kept his promises to the "Israel" of the Gentiles by a series of quotations from the Old Testament. This is more rabbinical interpretation, depending on the fullness of meaning disclosed by events. Hosea was referring to the "remnant" of Israel; however in Paul's interpretation the term is applied to the Jewish Christians. Paul then returns to his thesis that righteousness comes from faith, not from Law.

Paul now expands his thesis that the unbelief of Israel is not a failure of God but a failure of Israel (10:1-21). Once again he states his personal involvement. The Jews are not irreligious like the Gentiles; no, they have another and more serious failure. Most commentators think that when Paul speaks of "misguided zeal" (10:2) he is thinking of his own previous history. This comes dangerously close to worshiping the Law instead of God—a phrase which Paul does not use and probably would not use. But he does say that the Jews seek the righteousness of the Law instead of the righteousness of God (10:3). JB's version of 10:4 interprets and simplifies the verse. The Greek literally means that Christ is the end of the law; it may be deliberately ambiguous, meaning both the end in time (as in JB) and the end in purpose. Equivalently, this means that Christ is the fulfillment of the Law; the law does not acquire full reality and meaning until Christ comes.

The argument in the rest of chapter 10 is a chain of biblical texts interpreted by rabbinical methods; we notice how often Paul draws on his own rabbinical learning when he engages in discussion with Jews and about Jews. The quotation from Leviticus 18:5 might seem to oppose Paul's thesis; but he has already dealt with the impossibility of keeping the Law. The Law is an impossible burden. Faith is no such burden. And no man need perform the impossible in order to reach Christ. He need not mount the heavens (supported by Deuteronomy 30:12, which refers to the Law) nor descend to the underworld (very loosely supported by Deuteronomy 30:13, which refers to crossing the seas, and by merely verbal similarity in Psalm 107:26). Paul refers these texts to the incarnation of the pre-existent Christ and to his resurrection from the dead. No, all that the righteousness of faith demands is that one profess it; it is on your lips. This is supported by Deuteronomy 30:14, which refers to the Law. The verse mentions the heart, which contains faith, and the lips, with which one confesses. It is interesting, to say the least, that Paul uses texts which affirm that the Law is easy to show that faith is even easier. From Isaiah 28:16 he deduces no distinction between Jew and Greek, a distinction which Isaiah could not have made. With no little originality he applies the invocation of the name of the Lord Yahweh (Joel 3:5) to the name of the Lord Jesus for salvation.

Paul then turns to respond to several possible objections which might excuse Jews from responsibility (10:14-21). The first is that the gospel was not proclaimed; this demands not only an apostle, but an accredited apostle ("sent" 10:15). This is refuted from Isaiah 52:7, which in context refers to the announcement of the end of the exile. Another excuse is unbelief; Paul must mean that the unbelief of some is a temptation to others. This is refuted from Isaiah 53:1, a general allusion to unbelief. Another possibility is that the proclamation was not heard. This is refuted from Psalm 19:4, certainly used freely; the psalm refers to the revelation of God in nature. Finally, they heard but did not understand. This is refuted by texts which can be interpreted of the Gentiles (Deuteronomy 32:21; Isaiah 65:21) but which in the context actually refer to Israel, and by one text which does refer to Israel (Isaiah 65:2, parallel to 65:1, just quoted). Paul could, indeed, have piled up texts of the Old Testament which refer to the unbelief and obtuseness of Israel. Many scholars now think that he worked with a handbook of collected texts rather than with the entire Hebrew Bible, and that these texts were given in the Greek translation. To some degree, of course, Paul depended on his own memory; this was really the most important tool of scholarship for the rabbi.

Another objection remains to be answered, and it is the most serious of all: Has God rejected Israel (11:1)? This might be the first explanation which would occur to a Gentile. Paul denies it instantly with the somewhat strange reason that he, a Jew by nativity, could never accept this hypothesis. But this appeal to Scripture has implications, and the following verses show that he was aware of them. He appeals to the story of Elijah (I Kings 19), in which the prophet confesses that he has utterly failed to reach the Israelites. Yahweh answers that he has preserved seven thousand who have not worshipped the Baal. Paul calls this a "remnant," using the term from the prophetic literature which became a technical expression. "Remnant" in any hypothesis indicates a minority of the people, and Paul goes on to say this expressly in 11:17. The failure of the majority is again explained by a chain of biblical texts. The first two of these apply to Israel, but the third (Psalm 69:22-23) is extended to Israel by rabbinical interpretation. We do not know how many of the first Christians were Jews, but Paul clearly indicates that Jewish Christians were a very small proportion of the entire Jewish people.

Paul sees a providential purpose in the unbelief of the Jews (11:11-15); and this answers the question whether the "fall" of the Jews is permanent. The unbelief of the Jews is the occasion of the proclamation of the gospel to the Gentiles, who believe in it. This statement has implications to which Paul does not attend and to which he probably did not advert. It can hardly be seriously meant that the Gentiles are admitted to faith only as substitutes for the Jews, or that they would not have had the gospel preached to them if the Jews had believed it. He probably does mean that the entire Jewish people should have been the apostles of the Gentiles; but this consideration would hardly suit the context. The belief of the whole Jewish people could not be a lesser benefit than the belief of the remnant. And Paul does indeed see this. He contrasts the reconciliation of the world (with God) through the unbelief of the Jews with the conversion of the whole Jewish people, which will be "life from the dead" (JB "resurrection from the dead" says more than the Greek). The phrase is difficult; but the reconciliation of the world is obviously a wonder which surpasses all expectation, and life from the dead is an even greater wonder. They are not merely wonders but blessings; and Paul repeats his point that the Jews are a medium of blessing to the Gentiles.

Paul now turns to analogies to confirm his point (11:16-24). The first analogy is dough, the second is the tree. The word he uses is "holy"; in Jewish rites holiness, like uncleanness, was communicated by contact. If the dough was consecrated, any profane element which was added became holy. If the tree is holy—the example is easier to grasp—then its branches and fruits are holy. Jesus used a similar example of the good tree and the good fruit (Matthew 7:17-20). The holiness of the Jewish people lies in its origins, and it can never be lost. By association, it seems, Paul turns to another example of a tree and lingers on it; moreover, it is somewhat surprising to find so urban a man as Paul dwelling on this example. The practice of grafting branches on olive trees was known to farmers of the Hellenistic-Roman world. The olive tree normally reaches a great age, although tourists who hear that the olive trees of Gethsemane witnessed the agony of Jesus hear a fairly typical tourist exaggeration. The branches literally die while the tree continues to live; and when the young branches are grafted, they do not lose their youth but live by the vitality of the tree.

It is necessary for the analogy that the branches which have been lopped off are not really "dead," but capable of being regenerated by grafting, a wonder which was scarcely possible to the horticulturists of the Hellenistic-Roman world. And this feature is not merely accessory, for Paul insists that the lopping off of the "natural" branches is not a permanent separation. He warns the Gentiles that they too, the grafted branches, can die and be lopped off. The figure must not be pressed too closely; for what is the "tree" into which the branches are grafted? Paul would probably answer that the tree is the patriarchs, God's original planting. He has already affirmed that the Gentile believers are the children of Abraham not according to the flesh, but according to faith.

Paul now turns to the "mystery" behind all this; here, as elsewhere in Paul, "mystery" is a truth which is revealed only in the Christ-event. The mystery is that all of Israel will believe only after the "fullness" of the Gentiles (11:25) has believed. The meaning of "fullness" is not clear. The verse is in a strange way a commentary on the words of Jesus in Matthew 21:31; other Gospel passages express a similar thought less bluntly. What Paul calls a mystery is his personal conviction. The Jews have lost one of their privileges, the Messiah (9:5). He was of their flesh, and they should have been the first to believe in him and to proclaim him. Now they must wait for those to whom they should have proclaimed. Paul is sure that this waiting is not in vain.

To modern Jews this is the least pleasing word that Paul has spoken. They do not share his belief in the mystery and his conviction that the ultimate destiny of Judaism is faith in the "Messiah" in whom Paul believed. Paul believed that the gifts of God are irrevocable (11:29). Modern Jews agree with him in this, but do not consider faith in the Messiah as one of the gifts. These positions seem irreconcilable and to that extent the "mystery" of Paul is frustrated.

Paul closes this topic with a passage called by interpreters a hymn (11:33-36). The hymn is a praise of the inscrutable wisdom of God, which is the sole and ultimate explanation of all reality—"from him, through him, to him" renders the Greek more literally. And this hymn would be Paul's answer to the considerations which were raised in the preceding paragraph.

With chapter 12 Paul begins the moral exhortation which concludes this letter. We have seen that such moral exhortations are characteristic of the letters. Some scholars have suggested that chapter 12 should follow immediately after chapter 8; the discussion of the Jews, they think is a foreign body in the letter to the Romans. They do not think that it is written by another author. The suggestion has not been accepted by many scholars, and the question of why Paul dwelt on this subject in Romans remains unanswered.

The first exhortation (12:1-2) is quite general, but it does contrast the worship "worthy of thinking beings" with other rituals, Jewish or pagan. The statement is somewhat anti-ritual; and it must be remembered that the early church had no ritual worship which matched the ritual either of the Jerusalem temple or of the pagan temples. Naturally they had nothing to correspond to the splendor of later Christian ritual worship. Paul apparently would have been impressed with Christian ritual worship as little as he was with Jewish or pagan ritual.

The exhortations to humility and charity (12:3-13) do not respond to any situation in the Roman church, which was unknown to Paul. The allusions to "gifts" must be compared to I Corinthians 12-14; no one could serve the church except by virtue of a charisma. As at Corinth, these could be occasions of personal vanity. Paul enumerates seven such gifts (12:6-8). These could correspond to official functions within the church, but they probably do not; Paul did not know what the official structure of the Roman church was, and we have no reason to think that the early churches had a uniform official structure. The seven gifts mentioned here are concerned with instruction and almsgiving; these were the "works" of the early churches. The comparison of the church to the human body has no reference to the doctrine of the "mystical body of Christ" but employs a well-known analogy found also in pagan literature (cf. I Corinthians 12:12-26).

The exhortations to charity (12:14-21) may be compared to Matthew 5:28-48; however, the epistle to the Romans was written before the Gospel of Matthew. This primary point of Christian moral teaching came early in the church. Early also, and found in this passage, is the doctrine of nonresistance to evil, which goes further than the doctrine of nonviolence. Love of enemies forbids revenge; Paul presents this in the somewhat strange formula of "give place to the wrath" (12:19), meaning the wrath of God (which JB puts into the translation). This does not mean that the believer should pray for the wrath of God or desire it, but that he should simply allow it to work with no help or hindrance from himself. One should leave wrath to God; those good works which we can perform God leaves to us.

The words of Paul on submission to civil authority (13:1-7) have been much discussed and are easily misunderstood; it is necessary to understand them against their background in biblical literature and in the thought of Paul. The words are readily understood as a basis for the divine right of kings. However, Paul, who was, according to tradition, executed by the Roman government for disloyalty, was hardly the man to defend this thesis. When the epistle was written the Christians had experienced no opposition from the Roman government. Jesus had been executed by the Romans, but the Christians of Paul's time made no effort to assign blame for this (see chapters 9-11 above). In the world in which Paul lived, the Roman Empire was the only effective government known; and as an agent of peace and law and order it should not be underestimated. To the men of the first century the Roman Empire was almost a cosmic power rather than a political power, one of the constitutive principles of the universe. Jews and Christians refused to worship Caesar as god, but this text of Paul shows his recognition of the power of Caesar.

The idea of Rome as the bearer of the power of God and the representative of the power and justice of God—which seems to touch, as we have noticed, on the divine right of kings—must be seen against its bibilical background. Since the rise of Assyria as a world power in the eighth century B.C., the states of Israel and Judah had to deal with political powers of far greater magnitude than they had ever known before. The prophetic attitude toward such powers was expressed by Isaiah (for example, 5:26-30; 10:5-19) and Jeremiah (for example, chapters 25-29); the conquerors were the agents of the justice of God against the sinful kingdoms of Israel and Judah, and it was a sin to resist them. This principle in no way authenticated the moral character of the governments of the conquerors, and they themselves would be, in the course of God's mysterious providence, conquered and reduced to servitude by others. The duty of the believer was to submit to them as long as God allowed them to exercise power.

Paul really does not go beyond this prophetic teaching in his recommendations to Christians to accept the rule of Rome. Since Rome at that time had presented no threat to the Christian community, there was no reason for him to express hostility such as the writer of the Book of Revelation, for example, had expressed. His recommendations are simply practical; they are a way of dealing with an existing situation which the Christians could not change—they lack theoretical approval either of the Roman Empire or of any other political authority.

The primacy of the commandment of love is clearly expressed in 13:8-10, which should be compared with Matthew 22:34-40, written later than the Epistle to the Romans; but the teaching goes back to Jesus. The one commandment (Leviticus 19:18) fulfills the entire Law; Matthew joins to Leviticus 19:18 the commandment of the love of God (Deuteronomy 6:6), but takes the two commandments as one.

Paul's exhortation concerning "the time" (see JB note) reminds Christians that with the death and resurrection of Christ the last world age has begun. There will not be another act of God like this, and in this sense salvation is "nearer." It seems that the sense of an impending and near Second

Coming is less acute in this passage than in the earlier letters to the Thessalonians and the Corinthians. The urgency here is for moral reform. The antithesis between light/darkness—the eschatological images for good/evil—leads Paul to mention the vices of darkness, the revelry of excess in drinking and sex: We have already observed that the Christian moral teaching imposed a revolutionary restraint upon the accepted behavior patterns of the Hellenistic-Roman world.

The main part of the exhortation (14:1-15:13) is given in the topic discussed in I Corinthians 8-10—the problems of scandal to the "weak." The problem must have been more than minor in the early church, since it is discussed at length both in Corinthians and again in Romans; the church in Rome was unknown to Paul personally. Both treatments indicate that the apostolic church had more diversity than we readily recognize; and we are reminded that there was no structure of supreme authority which imposed uniformity upon the various churches. We know that most churches included Jewish Christians and Gentile Christians, which meant different observances in the two groups; and we have noticed the problems created by those who thought the Jewish observances were required even of the Gentiles. This, as we have seen, was very probably the major threat to unity in the apostolic church; and for this reason Paul gives it so much space and so much attention.

The basic principle of Paul's solution is the principle stated in I Corinthians; it is the duty of the "strong," the person who is better informed, to accommodate himself to the weakness of the ignorant and the timid. As we observed in I Corinthians, this does not mean that the strong should make no effort to instruct the weak; the emphasis is upon instruction. The strong should not treat the scruples of the weak as nonexistent or unimportant, and until an opportunity for instruction arises the strong should yield. Paul appeals to the sincerity which should be presumed in each Christian; the scrupulous person acts from a desire to honor and serve the Lord, and this desire must be respected. Since Paul is addressing the strong, he does not take the opportunity to remark that the weak should make the same presumption concerning the strong; it is a part of "weakness" that it is unable to rise to a tolerance of differences. To the weak everything is of equal importance, and Paul seems to think that the weak will remain in this error until they are instructed by the strong. As in I Corinthians, Paul lays the duty of tolerance and compassion upon those who believe that they are better instructed and more firmly grounded in the faith.

Two points may be noticed about Paul's position on this question. The first point is that it is in accord with Paul's rejection of the Law, in spite of an apparent inconsistency, to be noticed shortly. What "observances" did Paul think were obligatory? He mentions none, and we must take seriously his statement (in 13:8 above) that love of the neighbor fulfills all obligations. He mentions dietary observances, apparently going so far as complete abstinence from meat, and the observance of unspecified holy days. These suggest Jewish observances, but Paul is not as fierce in rejecting them as he is in rejecting circumcision and the observance of the whole Law in Galatians and in Romans 2-4 and 6-7. We conclude that such observances were not urged as obligatory upon all. They appear to have resembled modern devotional practices, which in modern church discipline cannot be presented as obligatory, but are often presented as quick ways to a higher level of Christian faith and Christian life. If this were included in the observances which Paul mentions he would, it seems, have been much less tolerant of the weak. The history of the church has long included the urge of many of its members to find some supplement to the gospel which promised salvation or perfection with a degree of assurance which is not found in the simple gospel. Such supplements generally have led to an elitism which is contrary to the unity to which Paul exhorts here.

The second point is that church unity for Paul admits a surprising degree of diversity. Unity did not rest upon uniformity of cult and discipline; and we have not reached the state at which unity of creed becomes vitally important. Had

Paul thought of unity in terms of discipline and cult he should have rejected vigorously the efforts to add to the gospel such things as dietary practices and holy days. He seems to regard these as aberrations—harmless, tolerable for the sake of unity.

The only church unity which Paul knows is the unity of love, which is not secured by uniformity of creed, cult or discipline. If Paul had had second sight into the future he would have known how much of church history would confirm his judgment. Speaking, as we noticed, to the strong, he points out that it is their duty to do nothing which will make it more difficult for the weak to sustain their faith, and they must be ready to accept some personal inconvenience for this. It is, of course, to be hoped that all will become strong. Paul does not believe that all will become strong if the strong insist on throwing their weight around.

Paul seems to be aware that an objector might ask whether he has not compromised the gospel of Christian freedom on which he has insisted in the first part of the epistle. If the Christian is free of the yoke of the Law, why should he then renounce his new freedom in favor of a servitude created by ignorance and timidity? In all candor Paul does not deal with this question directly. He seems to think that the tolerance of the strong will lead to a community in which Christian freedom is everywhere cherished amid the diversity of persons and cultures. Love, as we noticed, is the only effective agent of Christian unity and of Christian freedom. Freedom which is indifferent to the needs of others is not Christian freedom; this, and not the Law—nor a Christian substitute for the Law—is the only restraint upon Christian freedom. And in meeting the needs of others the Christian community is created. Paul supports his vision of Christian unity by a chain of Old Testament texts rabbinically interpreted (15:7-13). These texts are taken to predict a community of Jews and Gentiles living together in the worship of the one God.

The passage 15:14-31 very probably forms the conclusion of the epistle (see below); it falls into two parts. Paul first excuses himself once more for writing to a church which he did not found, and repeats that it is his general practice not to deal with the churches established by others. He excuses himself by appealing to the nature of his apostolic commission. He is the apostle of the Gentiles (Galatians 2:7); and this seems to imply rather decisively that the church of Rome was substantially Gentile. The JB translation "priest" (15:16) is inaccurate; the Greek word *hiereus,* priest, is never used of a church officer in the New Testament. Rather, the word which Paul uses means "minister," one who furnishes the material of the rite or assists in the rite. Paul likens his pagan converts to the victim which is presented to God in sacrifice.

Paul finds another excuse in the success of his mission to the Gentiles. He attributes this success to the work of Christ himself in Paul, especially in "signs and wonders." His progress has run from Jerusalem to Illyricum; the latter name designated the territory on the east coast of the Adriatic Sea, the modern Yugoslavia and Albania. It is hard to see why Paul should mention this obscure province if he had not been there.

Paul then speaks of his plans. The collection which he had taken up in Macedonia and Archea (see Galatians 2:10; I Corinthians 16:1-4; II Corinthians 8:1-9:15) must be delivered in Jerusalem; we have already suggested reasons why Paul thought he should do this personally. The collection would serve as a bond of union between the Jewish and the Gentile churches, and it would recommend Paul personally; he was surely not on the highest favor with the authorities of the Jerusalem church. He says he has no more work to do "here," which must mean not merely Greece, but the entire eastern Mediterranean region. Interpreters point out that this means that Paul considered it his mission to open new territory, not to maintain established churches or even to work out of them. He intends now to go to Spain, the extreme west of the Roman Empire; Britain was not yet within Paul's field of vision.

It is not known whether he ever made the journey. We are told in Acts that his arrest and imprisonment in Jerusalem delayed his arrival in Rome for several years. Only two ancient sources refer to a journey to Spain, and they could have drawn conclusions from this passage of Romans. The traditional date of Paul's death (67-68) would leave little time for an extended missionary journey to Spain.

The request for prayers in 15:30-33 has the appearance of a conclusion, and in all probability it is. There are good reasons for supposing that chapter 16 does not belong to the letter to the Romans. Paul mentions 26 persons by name, and sends friendly greetings to all with the possible exception of Aristobulus and Narcissus (16:10-11), whose households are greeted. Others are included but not named. No other letter has such a list, and interpreters remark that this is a large number of persons to greet in a place where Paul has never been. Furthermore, Epaenetus (16:6) is the first convert in Asia. Aquila and Prisca settled in Ephesus after the Jews were expelled from Rome in the reign of Claudius (A.D. 49; Acts 18:18; I Corinthians 16:19). These slender indications suggest that chapter 16 was addressed not to Rome but to Ephesus, where Paul had lived for three years.

It has been suggested that chapter 16 was attached to the copy of Romans which was sent to Ephesus. In Colossians 4:16 there is a reference to a circulation of letters beyond those to whom they were addressed. The letter also has the form of a letter of introduction for Phoebe; such letters are well-known from the Roman world. If this hypothesis is correct, the warning of 16:17-20 is addressed not to the Romans but to the Ephesians. The verses have a directness which is unlike the text of Romans, but easily understood in a letter written to those whom Paul knows well. The warning is too general for interpretation in detail. It is directed against the apostles of disunity, apparently those who add obligations to the gospel. This would reflect the disputes with Judaizing Christians; we remarked that Romans 14-15 is by contrast quite tolerant of "the weak." The blessing in 16:20 has the appearance of a conclusion; and here we are forced to admit that there is more disturbance in the text than the addition of a letter to Ephesus would cause; for the blessing is followed by personal greetings from the companions of Paul.

The names of Gaius and Erastus suggest that this was written in Corinth; this is in agreement with the place of composition both of Romans and of the letter to the Ephesians (chapter 16). Tertius wrote the only personal greetings from an amanuensis in the entire New Testament collection of letters. This also suits the address of this letter to Ephesus; if Paul was unknown in Rome, it is doubtful that Tertius would have inserted his name in a letter to strangers.

The doxology (16:25-27) is generally regarded as an addition both to the letter to the Romans and to the letter to the Ephesians. Its presence may be attributed to a scribe who noticed that in its final form the letter ended with personal greetings and not with the conclusion characteristic of Paul. The scribe found or composed this doxology and attributed it to Paul (16:25); but he did not succeed in writing it in the style of Paul.

Chapter Seven
EPISTLE TO THE PHILIPPIANS

The city of Philippi, named after Philip of Macedon, the father of Alexander the Great, lay in northeast Macedonia on the Via Egnatia, the Roman road from Italy to Byzantium. In the time of Paul it was a genuine "Roman" city, populated mostly by veterans from the Roman legions and subject to Roman law. The ethnic population of the city supports indications in the epistle that the church of Philippi was largely if not entirely Gentile. Paul's first visit is mentioned in Acts 20:6. These two passages give no information about the founding of the church, which appears to have been comparatively large and to have had close personal relations with Paul.

The quality of these personal relations appears when we look for the occasion of the letter. We have noticed that the letters to Thessalonica, Galatia, and Corinth were responses to problems of belief and discipline in these churches. The letter to Rome is a special case. The letter to Philippi mentions no specific problem, unless the concern about Epaphroditus (more below) can be called a problem. It certainly was not a problem of belief or discipline. A possible occasion may appear in the note of thanks to the Philippians (4:10-20).

Modern scholars have not reached an agreement on the date and place of composition of the letter. Paul wrote from imprisonment (1:13f, 20). Early interpreters easily connected this with the arrest and imprisonment of Paul which are related in Acts 21-28; the allusion to the *praetorium* (1:13) and to members of Caesar's household (4:22) supported this interpretation. The place of imprisonment was naturally identified with Rome. Certain difficulties in this interpretation led some scholars to suggest that the letter was written from Caesarea (Acts 23:23—26:32). This does not meet with all the objections, and contemporary opinion favors Ephesus as the place of composition. Acts mentions no imprisonment in Ephesus, but Paul refers several times to problems and perils in "Asia." Furthermore, he alludes in II Corinthians 11:23 to several imprisonments. Here as elsewhere the epistles are a more reliable source for the life of Paul than Acts.

The major difficulty with placing the epistle between Rome and Philippi is that, in ancient times, the journey would require a month. Yet the epistle implies about four journeys within a relatively short time between Philippi and the place where Paul was imprisoned. Caesarea is also remote enough to create the same problem. The journey to Ephesus, however, took only about a week. There is also a lack of consistency between Paul's plans after his release, which include a journey to Philippi, and his plans in the letter to Rome, which indicate a journey to Spain. This is not serious, and requires more consistency in Paul's plans than he need have shown.

Still another problem is created by the allusion to Jewish-Christian adversaries. If the letter had been written from Rome, it would have been in about 61-62. Most interpreters believe that the Jewish-Christian controversy was no longer acute at this date. Composition in Ephesus would put the letter about 56-57, earlier than Romans.

The reader will by now have become accustomed to references to the occasionally jerky composition of Paul's letters. This quality is so evident in the letter to Philippi that many interpreters have asked whether it is a letter or a conflation of several letters. The transitions at 2:19; 3:2; 4:10 are extremely abrupt, even for Paul. Yet no clear partition into separate letters appears. The letters which one could recover by division at the points mentioned would lack some of the formulae of introduction and conclusion (although 3:1 reads much like a conclusion). They would be short, at least as short as the letter to Philemon, which was a personal letter to an individual, not a letter to a church. One can only mention these suggestions, and recall that we must often explain the unevenness of Paul's letters by appealing to the possibility that the dictation was spread out over a prolonged period of time.

Paul associates Timothy with himself in the address, although Timothy has nothing to do with the contents of the letter. The church of the "saints" is addressed with its "elders and deacons." "Elders" (JB) is not altogether felicitous for the Greek *episkopoi;* but the translators are correct, with all modern commentators, in drawing attention to the fact that, at this time, these words did not have the meaning which their derivative, "bishops" and "deacons," had in the later hierarchical system. They were church officers, almost certainly of a committee type of administration, whose duties cannot be defined.

The thanksgiving and prayer (1:3-11) begin with an expression of joy. The joyful note continues throughout the letter; it is not unusual for Paul to express joy, even in such letters as Galatians and II Corinthians, but the expressions of this emotion are unusually frequent in Philippians. Unlike Galatians and II Corinthians, the letter has no complaint against the community; and the community is known to Paul personally, as the church of Rome was not. Paul's joy is based on the genuine faith and Christian progress of the Philippians. He speaks of their aid in propagating the gospel; this may refer to the monetary contributions they had made to Paul (see below), but far more probably it includes the positive work of preaching and instruction. These works were not limited to specialists. Paul's prayer is that the entire church at Philippi will continue to grow in love, which he has said elsewhere is the whole law (Rom 13:9-10) and the supreme spiritual gift (I Corinthians 13:1-13).

Paul's review of his personal situation (1:12-26) makes it clear that he is in prison, but he does not tell us why; presumably his correspondents knew. His imprisonment could hardly have been for preaching the gospel; this was not illegal, and Paul is glad that so many others are preaching the gospel. He gives no hint that they were in danger for illegal activities. Paul's preaching was, however, more than once an occasion of civil disturbances. In the incidents of this sort related in Acts the authorities seized the person against whom complaints were made in order to halt the disturbances, and released him after the trouble was over. In this case, however, Paul writes as if there was a serious threat to his life from a capital charge.

Paul's arrest was in some way a stimulus to preaching. He is happy at this and its apparent success, so much so that he does not care that some of the preachers speak from unworthy motives. Some preachers, it appears, had a personal hostility toward Paul. We have seen in other epistles that the apostolic church was not altogether a community of love. Clearly Paul is not charging these people with proclaiming a false gospel; they are authentic Christian missionaries, even if they are self-serving and mean of spirit.

Paul then begins what appears to be the earliest Christian meditation on martyrdom. The terminal of the Christian life is to be united with the Risen Lord in glory; as it is conceived in this passage, Paul is probably referring to a union with the Lord in the Parousia, his final appearance in glory. This was discussed in II Thessalonians. Paul now perceives that life is Christ and that death does not create the union but merely assures its permanence—if the word "merely" may be used of such a thing. The value of survival lies in the opportunity of further love and service, and love and service is life with Christ. If the love and service are achieved with suffering, this is most surely life with Christ in Christ.

In 1:27—2:18, Paul turns to exhortation; these are not rebukes but encouragements. He first encourages the Philippians to steadfastness in the faith. They can expect enmity and suffering. Paul does not specify the problem nor the enemies; Acts 17:1-15 tells of new difficulties raised against Paul and his companions by hostile Jews in the Macedonian cities. Paul then exhorts to mutual love, which must be based upon the renunciation of self-esteem. Christ is proposed as the model; this passage is the only place in the epistles of Paul in which the "imitation" of Christ appears.

The model (2:6-11) is one of the most intensely discussed passages of the epistles. The form of the lines is the form of the hymn. The lines contain an unusually large number of words which are not found elsewhere in the epistles of Paul; this has led scholars to conclude that Paul did not compose the hymn but quotes it from an early Christian liturgy. This is significant for the Christology of the primitive church; the Christology of the hymn is quite advanced beyond anything in the Synoptic Gospels, which it precedes, and as advanced as anything in the writings of Paul, of which it is independent. Christ is clearly a pre-existent being of divine status (v. 6). He "empties himself" by becoming man (v. 7), and suffers the ultimate humiliation of humanity—death by execution as a criminal of the lowest type (v. 8). God (not identified with Christ) has vindicated him by exalting him to heaven (v. 9) and by obliging the whole of creation to worship him (v. 10) and by declaring him Lord (Greek *kyrios*), a title which belonged in the Old Testament to Yahweh the God of Israel. The pre-existence is clear; the phrases of "divine state" and "equality with God" are not equally clear. "Divine state" is designated mostly in the New Testament by the title Son of God. The metaphor "emptying of self" (Greek *kenosis*) has no parallel in the New Testament; and the orthodox theology of Nicaea and Chalcedon was not couched in language which allowed the Incarnation to be conceived as a renunciation of divinity. If the hymn said the same thing in the same words as Nicaea and Chalcedon it would not be one of the most discussed passages of the epistles. The reader notices that the hymn skips over the resurrection and goes immediately to the exaltation. It is, as we said, advanced Christology; it is also primitive in the sense that it is in no sense an attempt to state the belief in the incarnation of a divine being in philosophical language, or even in careful language.

Christ is proposed as a model, however, not in his exaltation and lordship but in his refusal to cling even to that which was his inalienable right—"to empty himself" of the dignity and respect which was his due and to lay himself open to the deepest humiliation and the most painful death. This is the only road to glory which Paul knows, and he has hinted rather broadly in his opening paragraphs that it is the road on which he is trying to travel.

The final exhortation recommends acceptance of the obligations of the gospel without complaint or criticism. The tone of the letter does not imply that the Philippians themselves were among those who wished to rewrite the gospel, but it clearly implies that such had already appeared in the apostolic church. Paul again alludes to the danger facing him, and makes it a motive for the Philippians' fidelity to his teaching.

Abruptly, as we noticed, Paul turns to business. He is going to send Timothy and return Epaphroditus (with a name like that he had to be a Gentile convert), the messenger from Philippi. Most commentators think they see an implied question from Philippi: Where is our man Epaphroditus, and what has he been doing with the money we sent with him (4:10-20)? Paul seems to be saying that they should have trusted him; nothing happened except that the poor man fell ill, so receive him with kindness when he comes.

In another abrupt shift, Paul launches into a warning against Judaizing (3:2—4:1). His language is harsh. Commentators point out that Jews called pagans "dogs"; he turns the epithet upon them (3:2). Circumcision is dealt with in a pun which is in bad taste by modern polite standards (3:2 and JB note). Greek and Roman authors, whose language was usually broad, allowed themselves similar plays of wit. Paul then proceeds to go perhaps further than he has in any previous letter to reject his ancestral race and religion. He affirms, almost scornfully, that he is as Jewish as a man could be, born of the elite tribe of Benjamin, a Pharisee of strict observance, who proved his Jewish zeal by persecuting Christians; this is not said without sarcasm. He now counts this proud Jewish heritage as dung (more politely "rubbish" in JB 3:8). Somewhat carried away by the thought of what Christ has come to mean to him, he speaks with enthusiasm of knowing Christ and possessing Christ as the only values worth having. Christ is known by faith and possessed by suffering through which Paul learns the power of the resurrection. The Law promised the Jew "perfection," but it did not deliver its promise. Faith promises perfection and delivers it. Paul compares his pursuit of Christ to running a race, a figure used elsewhere in Galatians 5:7; I Corinthians 9:25. One need not think that Paul was a dedicated spectator of sports events. The games (mostly our track and field sports) were so common and so popular in the Roman world that sports metaphors entered into the common language, as they have into our own. The church of the second and third centuries became much less casual about Roman sports spectacles than Paul is in this passage. Roman tastes much preferred sporting with wild beasts and the murderous boxers and gladiators of the arena to the track and field competitions of the classic Greek games.

Paul recommends himself, not Christ, as a model of imitation (3:17); this is not vanity. Paul tried to live what he preached, and he does not seem to think that the imitation of Christ is within the reach of anyone. This is said in antithesis to the Judaizers, who worship the belly by attention to dietary laws and boast of their shame, that is, of circumcision of the genital organ. In contrast, the citizenship of Christians is in heaven (3:20). In this life they are travelers exiled from their homeland (see II Corinthians 5:1-8).

Another abrupt transition leads to some personal observations and some general exhortations (4:2-9). Two women, Evodia and Syntyche, have fallen into a serious quarrel, important enough to elicit a personal appeal. The JB translation of "Syzygus" as a personal name is unusual, since the name is found nowhere in Greek and Roman antiquity. The word means "yokefellow," and most translators and commentators render it as something like "partner." Paul uses this word nowhere else. The exhortations are quite general, but they return to the note of joy with which the letter began. It is striking that a short letter in which imprisonment and martyrdom are recurring themes should have a more joyful tone than any other letter of Paul.

There follows a note of thanks for a gift (4:10-20). Paul's policy on gifts and stipends has been discussed more than once in other letters. It is established that he supported himself by a trade; that he preached and taught without fee or stipend, a rabbinical tradition which he followed; that he intended no criticism of those who supported themselves only by preaching and teaching. We learn from this passage that he did accept gifts. He may not have accepted them except from people with whom he had firmly established personal relations. The words of 4:15-16 suggest that his relations with the Philippians were not like his relations with other churches precisely in his willingness to accept their gift. Other churches, he says, gave him nothing, and Paul did not ask for anything. It seems very likely that the church at Philippi was the first church to present him with an unsolicited and unexpected gift, and that this gave them a position of privilege; he would always take a gift from them because they put him at no disadvantage. It may seem ungracious to respond to a gift by saying that it is your friendship more than the gift that I value. This is a very weary modern cliche which Paul could utter and the Philippians could hear with no affection on either side. Paul means that grateful as he is for their gift and their friendship, his work as an apostle does not depend on whether he continues to receive gifts or not. If Paul could be slightly vain at times, one of the points of vanity was his ability to take hard knocks and still get his job done. It is a rather common form of vanity among people who work hard and know it.

"Caesar's household" (4:22) does not imply a Roman origin of the letter. It means almost the same thing as "government employees." It is rather curious that this group should send greetings to Philippi; it must have included a number of former Philippians.

Chapter Eight

EPISTLE TO THE EPHESIANS

The first question which arises concerning this epistle is whether it was addressed to Ephesus. "In Ephesus" is missing in the critical text of 1:1 (see JB note). According to Acts 20:31, Paul had spent three years at Ephesus; it is quite surprising that no name is mentioned in the letter except the name of Tychicus, the bearer. It is even more surprising that the letter has such an impersonal tone. When one compares this with all the preceding letters addressed to churches Paul knew, one has to wonder whether this was from Paul and whether it was addressed to Ephesus. Both questions are answered by many scholars in the negative. The absence of the name in the inscription has led many to think that the epistle was a circular letter addressed to a number of churches; the name of the church was filled in where the name "Ephesus" stands in the received text. As we shall see, the epistle bears on no particular problem of belief or discipline.

Doubts about the Pauline authorship are based principally upon the style, which is much more ponderous than the style of the letters which are certainly Pauline. There are a number of words peculiar to this letter, and most of them occur in just those parts which are somewhat different from the Pauline letters in doctrine; difference does not mean that this epistle contradicts the other epistles, but that it has lines of development which the other epistles do not have. The problem is complicated by the relation which exists between Ephesians and Colossians. Both in vocabulary and in context these two letters have an affinity with each other which is found nowhere else in the Pauline collection. Many think that

Ephesians was expanded from Colossians.

These considerations forbid one to believe that Paul produced Ephesians in the same way in which he produced I Corinthians. They do not forbid one to say that he had anything to do with Ephesians. But if one insists that Paul is the "author" of Ephesians, he must also be ready to admit that Paul commissioned the writing instead of doing it himself. One must further admit—we presuppose certain problems not yet considered—that the one to whom he commissioned the writing was either the author of Colossians or had Colossians as a model and a source.

These problems obviously make it quite difficult to determine the date and the place of composition of Ephesians. It is one of the "captivity epistles" (3:1; 4:1; 6:20). If it is attributed directly to Paul, the problems of the date are the same as the problems of the date of Philippians. If it is not from Paul, then the author is committing a literary fiction which does not appear necessary. This seems to support the opinion that Paul did not dictate the epistle but commissioned its writing.

The greeting is brief and impersonal (1:1-2); as we have noticed, it is probable that Ephesus was not in the original text. The blessing, on the contrary, is long, and it contains material which, in both content and style, is different from the Pauline letters (1:3-14). It is couched in the style of the hymn, which the JB translation shows by its arrangement of lines. The hymn celebrates the saving plan of God which was formed from creation. This plan incorporates a "mystery" (v. 9), which in Ephesians means the plan to bring all men together under one head, Christ (v. 10); that is, to extend to the Gentiles the salvation which was first offered to the Jews. This distinction is meant by the "we" of verse 11 (the Jews) and the "you" of verse 13 (the Gentiles). It is thought by many commentators that the language of the hymn reflects the formula for baptism used in the early church. In such formulae, what the candidate was expected to believe was set forth at some length. The declaration of the equality of Jews and Gentiles, however, was hardly a part of the formula for baptism. Such a statement as this would have been quite meaningful in the Hellenistic-Roman cities of the empire, into which streamed vast numbers of people who had no real bonds of union with each other either through community of tribe or even community of language. The headship of Christ offered a vision of human community which the Roman Empire did not offer.

The prayer which follows (1:15-23) is a prayer for knowledge and understanding, which is a peculiarly Greek virtue. What the author asks in prayer is a knowledge of what God has accomplished in Christ and what he will accomplish in the believer. What he has completed in Christ is the resurrection and the exaltation. The reference to "sovereignty, authority, power or domination" (1:21) does not exclude the political powers which rule the human community, but it is not limited to them; in short, it means the cosmic powers, not precisely angelic or demonic and not precisely excluding these either. In later Jewish belief the great political powers were seen as manifestations of hidden cosmic powers; without the support of such powers, the political powers could not endure. The cosmic character of these powers is clearer in Colossians. The cosmic dominion of Christ is clear in the identification of his body not only with the church but with all of creation; for it has not reached its "fullness" until his body fills all creation.

The gift of salvation to the Gentiles is a free gift of grace (2:1-11). The author again contrasts Jew ("I" in 3:2) with Gentile ("you" in 3:1). The Gentiles were slaves to the cosmic power (3:1). The Jews were not enslaved in the same way (slavery to the cosmic power is identified with idolatry), but they were enslaved to their own concupiscence. There is no distinction between Jews and Gentiles in salvation, for each of them are saved by the free gift of grace. Paul does not take the trouble to refute the claim that the Law was an agent of salvation.

Paul now moves to a vision of unity which was not common in the early church. Himself a Jew, he was reared in Jewish exclusiveness. The Jews were the people of God, the people of the covenant and the promise. They owed it to God and to themselves to keep themselves from corruption by mixing with the Gentiles, who were "without Christ, without hope, without God" (2:12). All this is ended by the cross and the blood of Christ; he has made of the two peoples one, one New People, one Body. Thus the Gentiles are no longer aliens and outsiders to the people of God; they enjoy full citizenship (see Philippians 3:20). By a change of figure, he makes them components of the building which is being erected. This building is the church, for it has apostles and prophets as its foundation and Christ as its cornerstone; the architectural metaphors of the writer are not created from a deep understanding of the craft. But the metaphor is not intended to be exact; this building grows, like a body.

The author now speaks of his own apostolate to the Gentiles (3:1-13; see Galatians 2:7). He calls himself a messenger of the "mystery" rather than a messenger of the gospel, the usual phrase in the Pauline epistles. The mystery is explicitly defined; it is the secret plan of God to deal with all men on the same level, not to maintain the difference between a chosen people and the reprobate mass of humanity. One must reflect briefly on this to see that what is said so casually goes far beyond what Paul said in Galatians and Romans. This particular development is one of the features of the epistle which makes interpreters wonder whether it is directly from Paul. The plan has been kept secret from the cosmic powers (3:9). The prayer of the author (3:14-21) is uttered on behalf of the Gentiles, and it reflects Greek rather than Jewish patterns of thought. Commentators point out that "the breadth, the length, the height and the depth" (3:18) are Stoic terms. When Christ lives in the Gentiles, he really becomes a new cosmos, a new "fullness" (31:9). It is also a Greek idea that the Gentiles should reach this fullness through "knowledge" (3:19).

Chapter four begins the exhortatory part of the epistle which continues to the end. The exhortation begins with a plea for unity. Seven principles of unity are enumerated; in the apostolic church it occurred to no one to include in such an enumeration the unity of government and structure.

Unity is affirmed in order to make room for a statement of diversity which does not destroy unity. The diversity of gifts is supported by a rabbinical interpretation of Psalm 68:18; the ascent and the descent probably refer to the Incarnation of the pre-existent Christ. If the enumeration of gifts is compared with Romans 12:3-8 and I Corinthians 12:1-31, an interesting difference appears. The gifts mentioned here are all clearly "official," in the sense that they are attached to permanent offices. The author does not mention the occasional charisma given to the faithful, or even such a charisma possessed habitually. Commentators think this may reflect a more closely organized church with a fixed hierarchical structure than we see in the churches founded by Paul. The point at issue, however, is that diversity of gifts and of office should not endanger the unity of the church, which is like a body with different members. The image of the body again is treated somewhat differently from the image in Romans 12:3-8 and I Corinthians 12:12-30. Here it is the body of which Christ is the head. By an anatomical analogy hardly valid according to modern standards, the head is considered as the source of the one life of the body from which life is dispensed to the various members, which are no less living with the one life because they have lower functions than some other member.

The moral exhortations (4:17—5:20) hew to basic moral issues with nothing eccentric or even peculiarly Christian. The author refers to the moral corruption of the pagan world, the same theme which is treated at greater length in Romans 1:18-32. One who does not know the moral level of the Roman world does not readily perceive what a revolutionary change in personal life and habits was demanded of those who believed the gospel. To call this "putting on a new man" was not an unreasonable exaggeration. The exhortation to put on the new man may be allusion to the baptismal ceremony in which the candidate stripped for baptism and then put on a clean white garment. The believers are warned against lying, anger, stealing, foul talk, spitefulness and grudges. The imitation of God and Christ (5:1-3) actually refers to the virtue of forgiveness (4:32); the chapter division obscures this.

We have had occasion in earlier epistles to refer to the sexual license of the Hellenistic-Roman world, and to observe that the New Testament is remarkably restrained on this topic. Ephesians 5:3-17 is an exception to this general restraint. This does not imply that the tone of the passage is frantic; it is simply a longer warning than one usually finds against sexual license. The author does not even want the topic mentioned—not that conversation is the same as the act, but it is not "becoming" for the saints. Prolonged discussion of this topic betrays an interest which the author would not find entirely healthy. The author adds a warning against excessive drinking, which tends to relax one's habitual inhibitions. Rather than the noisy carousing of revelry the believers should, if they must sing, sing the psalms and hymns of the liturgy. We have noticed that the type of community worship which we must suppose at Corinth would serve the purpose of community celebration as well as the purpose of community worship. The works of sex are, of course, the works of darkness. The saying with which Paul counters this (5:14) is found in no literary source, and scholars have concluded that it comes from an early Christian hymn.

By an easy transition the author turns to the topic of Christian marriage; he has produced a quite unusual treatment (5:21-33). The image of marriage as analogous to the union of Christ and the church appears in II Corinthians 11:2; and one may trace the theme back to the prophets Hosea, Jeremiah, Ezekiel, and II and III Isaiah, who represent Israel as the bride of Yahweh. The modern reader is at once struck by the fact that in this treatment love is the virtue of the husband and obedience the virtue of the wife. This surely reflects a Jewish background. At the same time, Paul considers the love of Christ for the church to be the love of total devotion to the point of self-abnegation; it is certainly not an expression of the ancient view of marriage as ownership of the wife by the husband. The modern reader may wonder why the author does not recommend such love to the wife. In his social context the author would not think that a woman was capable of exhibiting such love, for society did not give her the freedom to express such love; she could receive it, and this was her virtue. It is scarcely a model of marriage that has become completely archaic. The "mystery" of 5:32 is the revelation that the text of Genesis 2:24 refers not only to man and wife but to Christ and the church. The church "without speck or wrinkle" (v. 27) is neither the eschatological church, nor—certainly—the historical church; it is the church baptized, cleansed from sin and endowed with a new life. In ancient as in modern times the bride appeared in unspoiled beauty.

The other family relations are children-parents and slaves-owners (6:1-9). In neither of these relationships does the author mention love, and in this he again echoes his culture. According to Roman law, children were practically on the level of slaves, and slavery was chattel slavery. Respect and obedience are recommended to children and slaves, and kindness is suggested to parents and owners. Parents who did not flog their children and owners who did not flog or kill their slaves denied themselves a liberty which the law accorded them. This is less than revolutionary, and many have found the New Testament laggard in its casual acceptance of slavery. This will come up again when we treat the letter to Philemon.

The allegory of the spiritual war is somewhat drawn out (6:10-20). The details of the allegory are a chain of biblical allusions. The author refers again to the cosmic powers, "sovereignties and powers"; we have already observed that these are not simply the diabolical agents of popular belief, but superhuman powers who touch human life through nature and through politics. Against such beings unregenerate man is helpless. He must be armed with the power of God, and the power of God is the virtue with which God equips the believer. The conclusion, as we mentioned, is too brief and impersonal to be recommended as the writing of Paul to friends.

Chapter Nine
EPISTLE TO THE COLOSSIANS

The city of Colossae lay in the valley of the Lycus river about 110 miles east of its much more populous and important neighbor, Ephesus. It was a center of the textile industry, and seems to have experienced an economic depression similar to the depression which afflicted the centers of the New England textile industry in a much later period. Another neighbor, Laodicea (2:1, 4:16), was more prosperous than Colossae. The city was not evangelized by Paul himself but by his disciple Epaphras (4:12). This gave Paul the right to regard the church as his own; we have already adverted to his policy of not dealing with churches which he had not himself founded. Although Epaphras is a nickname for Epaphroditus, it is generally agreed that Epaphras was not the Epaphroditus of Philippi (Philippians 2:25-30). The name, which indicates a devotion to the goddess Aphrodite, seems to have been common in the Hellenistic world.

The Pauline authorship of the letter has often been questioned, but less frequently in contemporary scholarship. The style, as we remarked concerning the style of Ephesians, is rather heavy compared to the letters of Paul. The vocabulary contains a number of words not found in the Pauline epistles; this, however, may be explained by the fact that the letter deals with problems which do not occur in the other letters. We shall come to this very shortly. The problem of authorship is connected with the relation of Colossians to Ephesians; there is a community of themes and vocabulary between these two letters which appears nowhere else in the Pauline corpus. Modern opinion favors the view that Ephesians was written from Colossians as a source and a model. We have already remarked that Ephesians is viewed by many commentators as a circular letter addressed to several churches. If these churches were all in Asia Minor, it is quite probable that the theological problem of Colossae was found in other churches of the region as well. The problem of authorship, then, is simply the problem of whether Paul was able to deal with a problem which he did not treat in the other letters. If the question is put in these terms, then it is at once evident that there is no reason to deny that Paul could deal with a problem which he does not treat elsewhere, and that he could deal with it in different terms. At the same time, this involves a very fundamental problem, the problem of Christology. If Colossians is to be attributed to Paul, then one must stipulate that his Christology was advanced by reflection on the problem of Colossae and probably of other churches in Asia as well.

The problem of Colossae was some form of the doctrine called Gnosticism. This doctrine, of which a large number of variations arose, was more prevalent during the second and third centuries A.D. than at the time of Paul, and it is only recently that Gnosticism of this early period has been recognized. It is neither Jewish nor Oriental, but in many instances a strange mixture of the two streams. The name "Gnosticism" is derived from the Greek word for knowledge. Gnosticism in all its forms placed salvation neither in faith nor in love nor in the saving act of God in Christ but in the knowledge of a secret revelation, not found in the New Testament except in cryptic symbols which were understood only by the key given to some later prophet. The knowledge is the revelation of a system of intermediate beings through which God approaches man; of these intermediate beings, Christ is the greatest. Gnosticism generally exhibited a system of dualism which identified the powers of darkness and evil with the material component of the universe; the salvation of man consisted in his disembodiment, for only the soul can be saved and united with God. Ultimately salvation in Gnostic systems was a kind of absorption in God which at best can hardly be distinguished from pantheism.

All this is a rather ponderous package to read into Colossae in the 50s or 60s of the first century A.D., and no one thinks that the Gnosticism of Asia Minor was as advanced as the Gnosticism of the second century. Developed Gnosticism was not only a parody of the gospel, it was a denial of the gospel; and Paul does not take it as seriously as he took the danger created for the gospel by the Judaizers. But modern scholars believe that they can recognize a primitive Gnosticism at Colossae, and we deal with the epistle on this assumption.

Colossians is another of the "captivity epistles," and the problem of which captivity is referred to occurs in each one; it need not be the same captivity in each. We have seen that it is doubtful that Ephesians came from Paul himself; but if it came from his commission, then it is hardly possible to believe that this was a captivity in Ephesus, as most assume for Philippians.

There is, however, a connection between Colossians and Philemon, which may have been sent in the same dispatch. The dispatch could have come from Rome. Many commentators think that the developed Christology of Colossians implies a later date for the letter. If the problem was met for the first time, such a later date is not demanded. The letter to Philemon includes a request for lodgings when Paul arrives. Such a request is much more likely from Ephesus than it is from Rome.

Paul associates Timothy with himself in the brief greeting (1:1-2). The thanksgiving and prayer (1:3-14) make it clear that Epaphras and not Paul himself has been the missionary of Colossae. The Colossians are congratulated for their progress; already they manifest the Christian triad of faith, love and hope (1:4). The prayer seems to be directed to the particular needs of the Colossians; Paul asks that they may receive "knowledge," which is precisely that in which the Gnostics placed their salvation. All the knowledge that is needed is the knowledge of the will of God (1:9); and the will of God is his will to save all men through Christ. The knowledge of this is the totality of wisdom and spiritual understanding; it is the fullness of life and of strength. In this knowledge they are delivered from darkness into the realm of light. Darkness and light were Gnostic motifs, derived from the cosmologies of ancient Near Eastern religions. The phrase "kingdom of the Son" (1:13) is unusual in Paul, and it does not arise from the refutation of Gnosticism.

The proclamation of Christ as the head of creation (1:15-20) is thought by many interpreters to be a quotation from an early liturgical hymn. If it is, it shows an "advanced" Christology, as the hymn in Philippians 2:6-11 does. The two hymns each have some features of naivete which embarrassed later theologians—here, the statement that Christ is the first-born of all creation. This is immediately clarified by giving Christ the absolute priority over all creatures, not in time but in dignity; they are all created "in" him and "through" him. Biblical language was unable to make anyone but the Father the agent of creation; to the Son is given an instrumental role shared with no one else. He is also the primary purpose of creation, the one who explains all of reality; he is the principle of cosmic unity who sustains all reality in order.

This is clearly the pre-existent Christ. The priority which is his in creation is also his in the new creation. As the world was created in him and through him, so the church is created in him and through him. He is the first-born of the regenerate race, those whom God raises from the dead. He is the head of the new creation which is his body. His instrumentality is reconciliation rather than creation, and he achieves this by his death on the cross.

In the hymn we meet the cosmic powers mentioned in Ephesians—thrones, dominations, sovereignties, powers. These are not here mentioned as evil powers; rather, they are mentioned because they are no less subject to the priority of Christ than other creatures, and they have no share in the worship which is given him. He is the compendium of all creation; its "fullness" (JB, "perfection") is found in him (1:19).

There is really no source, biblical or extrabiblical, for this recital. It goes beyond Old Testament sayings concerning the word of God and wisdom of God. It goes far beyond the view of Christ as the new Adam (Romans 5). It does give reason for asking why it appears only here in the Pauline letters.

Paul applies the hymn to the Colossians, reminding them of what they were and what they have become. The words are more easily understood of a Gentile congregation. Like the church of Ephesians 5:26-27, the Christians at Colossae have become holy, pure and blameless. This condition can be maintained by perseverance in the faith; Paul prepares for the polemic which is to follow.

The reference made to filling up the sufferings of Christ (1:24, literally, "what is lacking of the sufferings of Christ") is rhetorical rather than dogmatic. What is lacking of the sufferings of Christ is the suffering of the members of his body; they, like him, must reach glory through suffering (Romans 8:17; Philippians 3:10-11). Paul has suffered as an apostle. Here again he speaks of the "mystery" rather than the gospel. The mystery is God's plan to save all mankind; but the mystery is incorporated in Christ himself. He is the wisdom (1:27), the knowledge (2:3). These words echo, as we have noticed, the language of the Gnostics. There is no occult knowledge by which salvation comes; the revelation of Christ is the revelation of the ultimate mystery of all wisdom and knowledge. What Paul's "struggle" (1:29—2:1) on behalf of the churches of the Lycus valley may have been we do not know; "struggle" is not a word which Paul would use lightly for dispute.

The polemic against errors is sustained through 2:6—3:4. The opening statement affirms the "Christocentric" character of the faith; Christ is the revelation of the truth of God; in him God accomplishes his saving act, and in him the fullness of creation is achieved. Paul warns against the deceptions of "philosophy"—the only occurrence of this word in the New Testament. It is a rather flattering word for Gnostic speculation, if Paul is referring to Gnostic theories. The JB translation "principles of this world" (2:8, 20; see the same phrase in Galatians 4:3) somewhat obscures the interpretation of many commentators who think that this phrase designates the cosmic powers already mentioned, who were personal beings, identical with the angels of 2:18 below. In Christ the fullness of divinity dwells "bodily" (2:9). This is an extremely obscure phrase; it may allude to the common Gnostic belief that divinity was filtered down in creation through the various grades of intermediate beings. The filtering was actually conceived as a lessening of divinity as the materiality of the beings increased, until in man only a spark was left. In Christ it is all there without any filtering. In language which echoes Romans (see JB margin), Paul states the union of the believer with Christ; it is not done by the Gnostic dematerialization, but by putting off the old man of "flesh" (the principle of mortality and sin) and putting on the new man of the Spirit (the phrase is not used here). Christ's death annuls the debt of human guilt and thus—we are not told how—takes away the power which the cosmic beings wield over men. The powers are hitched behind the chariot of the triumphant Christ like defeated kings in the triumphal procession of a victorious Roman general.

Paul now warns against the vain observances of rites (2:16-23). He does not specify what they are. If they are Jewish observances, this is the only place in the epistles where he refrains from identifying the observances from which Christians are released. It is probable that these rites were a Gnostic conglomeration of pagan and Jewish rites. Certainly the new moon and the Sabbath were Jewish festivals. Dietary laws were Jewish, but there were other dietary laws in the world of Hellenistic religions. In some Greek philosophical schools ascetical discipline was practiced. In general, Paul is simply not ascetical; he is not explicitly opposed to ascetical discipline, but he never recommends it and makes it no part of the obligations of the Christian life. He says that dietary practices are simply human. He admits that they have a superficial attraction ("wisdom," 2:23), but denies that they have any lasting effect.

The worship of angels (2:18) seems to be the worship of the cosmic powers. Later Judaism, however, showed a great interest in angels, illustrated in such late books as Daniel and Tobit, and even more in Jewish apocryphal books, which contain elaborate speculations on the angelic world. It is from such speculations that the traditional names of the archangels (of whom the apocryphal authors counted seven) in Christian folklore are derived. Paul is deeply concerned about anything which would seem to interfere with the unique mediation of Christ. In later Judaism the interest in the angels was a part of the religious attitude which made God more and more remote. In Christ, God came as close to man as is conceivable. Paul wished neither the angels nor the cosmic powers to come between man and God.

The fleshly quality of the observances leads Paul to tell the Colossians to raise their minds from an earthly to a heavenly level. He told the Philippians (3:20) that their citizenship is in heaven. Already the Colossians live in Christ, but that life is hidden because Christ is raised above the earth. In the Parousia, his glory and theirs will be revealed.

There follows a moral exhortation (3:5—4:1); commentators think that this and similar passages may be related to the instruction given before baptism. The fact that there are three groups of five suggests that a mnemonic device may be found here. The first group of five vices is opposed, except for greed, to chastity (3:5). The second group includes sins of anger and faults of the tongue (3:8). The catalogue of five virtues (3:12) is concerned with fraternal relations. These are based on the principle of Christian unity, which annihilates all ethnic and social distinctions (3:11). This may be compared with Galatians 3:28; both statements are as sweeping as they could be in the world of Paul. The enumeration suggests a Gentile congregation.

Without using the phrase, Paul tells the Colossians that they are the new Israel—"the chosen race, the saints." The mark of the new Israel is not life under the Law but life in love, which will create peace.

The morality of the family is briefly treated (3:18—4:1). We have dealt with the social background of the recommendations in discussing Ephesians; love is the duty of the husband, submission the duty of the wife. For some reason the instructions to the slaves are given at greater length than the instructions to the masters. It must have been difficult for a chattel slave to see Christ the Lord in the owner who had the freedom to dispose of the life and death of his slaves.

Paul asks for prayers and makes a suggestion, unusual in the epistles, that the Colossians should use tact and prudence in conversing with unbelievers. He recognized that there could be no greater recommendation of the gospel than those who believed in it.

The conclusion is rich in personal names. Two of them are counted among the evangelists, Mark and Luke; there is no suggestion that either of them had written a gospel or was thinking of writing one. Onesimus must be the slave concerning whom Paul wrote to Philemon. The letter is to be sent to Laodicea in exchange for the letter which Paul wrote to Laodicea; some have thought that this letter to Laodicea is our Ephesians, or a version of it. It is somewhat sad that Paul recognizes that only two Jewish Christians remain in his company; we have seen indications that this division in the apostolic church may have been much deeper than the documents tell us.

Chapter Ten
PASTORAL EPISTLES

The title "pastoral epistles" applies to 1-2 Timothy and Titus. The title is well given; these letters are addressed to individuals who have a pastoral office over local churches, and they deal with the way in which this office is to be administered. We speak of "pastoral office" because we cannot define the responsibility. Timothy and Titus do not appear as bishops in the sense in which Ignatius of Antioch (d. 107) was a bishop; they do not head a local church, but appear as legates of Paul and general overseers of several churches—Titus over the churches in Crete. They are not apostles and the office described has no successors in the modern church.

Timothy is mentioned in the book of Acts as having accompanied Paul on the second and third missionary journeys. Paul associates Timothy with himself in the greetings of 2 Corinthians, Philippians, Colossians, 1-2 Thessalonians, and Philemon; he is mentioned several times in 1-2 Corinthians and certainly was closely associated with Paul in the evangelization of Corinth. Titus, on the other hand, is not mentioned in Acts; he is mentioned in Galatians and 2 Corinthians, and he was sent to Corinth as Paul's representative during the troubled period between the two Corinthian epistles. Titus was a Gentile; Timothy, the son of a Gentile farmer and a Jewish mother, was a Jew by Jewish interpretation.

The majority of modern interpreters do not think the letters were written by Paul or at his commission. They are regarded as pseudonymous letters; this question was touched upon in our introduction to the epistles. That they cannot be fitted into the life of Paul as we know it is not decisive; nothing is known of his life after A.D. 62, and the tradition that he was executed in the persecution of Nero in 68 is hardly as well founded as the tradition that Jesus was executed in Jerusalem under Pontius Pilate. The best argument for his death in Rome is that no other city claimed it. Other reasons for the doubtful authorship should be briefly set forth.

As for other doubtful letters, there are numerous and obvious differences between the pastoral epistles and the surely Pauline epistles in style and vocabulary. In the pastoral epistles these can be perceived even in translation; and they seem to be decisive for the position that Paul did not dictate these letters as he dictated Galatians and 1-2 Corinthians —that is, he can only have commissioned their writing. In this hypothesis, however, one encounters two other problems. One is the insistence of the epistles on "sound doctrine." This is simply never proposed in the certainly Pauline epistles, which show no interest in "doctrine." The idea of orthodox doctrine cannot be shown before the postapostolic period. Some interpreters argue from the nature of the errors which the writers confute. This is less convincing, for we know very little of the errors which the apostolic church had to meet. It must be admitted that these errors do not appear in the Pauline epistles. The second problem is the interest of the epistles in church structure. Many interpreters argue that this structure must be postapostolic. This again is less convincing, for the structure of the apostolic church is nearly totally unknown. The structure reflected is not that of the monarchical bishop, the priests and the deacons which appears in the letters of Ignatius of Antioch; this suggests that the pastoral epistles are earlier than the epistles of Ignatius. Yet it remains true that the Pauline letters tell us nothing of the structure of the churches. It is difficult to assume that if Paul were interested in ecclesiastical structures, the interest would appear only in these epistles.

These considerations impose the conclusion that the part of Paul in the composition of these epistles was not the same as his part in the composition of the surely Pauline letters. They do not impose the conclusion that the pastoral epistles were produced by the school of Paul, by which we mean a group of disciples, nameless for us, who preserved and edited his letters and felt themselves entitled to produce writings under his name.

Some interpreters who do not accept Paul's authorship of the pastoral epistles believe that the epistles contain material which did come from Paul directly, and that the Pauline scribes expanded this matter into its present form. Since it is not possible to sort out the Pauline materials, this theory is not strongly recommended. With or without such materials, the scribes of the school felt that they were expressing the mind of Paul faithfully.

The greeting (1:1-2) is standard, except that it is addressed to an individual. Chapter 1, verse 3 suggests that the destination was Ephesus; but this may be part of the literary fiction. The first charge to Timothy is to arrest false teaching. The teaching is not described, but "myths and endless genealogies" (v. 4) suggest the type of material which is found in Jewish apocryphal books. These books also contain speculations about heavens and angels. Such speculation seems idle rather than heretical, and relatively harmless; certainly Christians have been indulging in such speculation since the pastoral epistles were written. They do distract from the main purpose, which is love (1:5). The author is not replacing one speculation with some other speculation; he seems to have no use for speculation at all.

The false teachers seem to be Jewish Christians (1:7); but we have noticed earlier that some modern interpreters think that these may be Gentile Christians who, to borrow and adapt a modern phrase, wished to be more Catholic than the church. The Jewish element in primitive Christianity seems to have impressed many Gentiles; and the original church was entirely Jewish. The statement on the Law (1:8-11) is probably dependent on the treatment of the subject in Galatians and Romans, but the author goes beyond these treatments. Paul said that the Law gave no power to fulfill its obligations. This writer says that the Law is only for sinners, not for "good people." This rephrasing is open to misunderstanding; it needs the explicit statement of Paul that love fulfills the law

The autobiographical allusions (1:12-17) contain nothing which could not be gathered from the Pauline epistles. The purpose of the allusions is to support the statement that Christ Jesus came into the world to save sinners—a statement which is most easily understood of the pre-existent Christ. If Christ could save Paul, he could save anyone; the statement is so disarming that one is tempted to regard it as genuinely autobiographical. The thought of this saving act elicits a doxology (1:17) of a type common in the Pauline epistles.

The "instructions" to Timothy (1:18-20) have a strange lack of clarity; the preceding material makes it likely that he is to adhere to sound doctrine. The author alludes to the part played by charismatic persons (prophets) in the rite of ordination. The names Hymenaeus and Alexander both occur in 2 Timothy. The language used concerning them is much more severe than that used by false teachers. "Handing over to Satan" probably means imprecations for such things as illness.

The directions for public prayer (2:1-8) emphasize prayers for public authorities; but no one is to be excluded from these prayers. No hostility toward the authorities of the Roman Empire is reflected here; one need only compare these lines with much of the Revelation of John to see the difference. The epistle seems to know no extended and severe persecution. The motivation for the prayer is the unity of God and the unity of humanity, linked by the one mediator, Christ Jesus. The commission of Paul as apostle to the Gentiles is equivalently a commission to proclaim the gospel to all humanity.

The directions concerning women (2:9-15) are offensive to modern women, and no wonder. We have observed earlier that in speaking of women, Paul—and the author of Timothy—reflects his Jewish rather than his Hellenistic background. First, the author prescribes modesty in dress and restraint in adornment. This was written in the culture in which wealthy women wore the *Coa vestis,* the famous weave from the isle of Cos which was nearly transparent.

Women are excluded from teaching and the exercise of authority. This is based on theological argument. The priority of the male reposes on the prior creation of the male and on the fall of the woman into sin before man. Woman is blamed for the fall in Sirach 25:24. The salvation of woman through childbearing is an allusion to Genesis 3:16, where the pangs of birth are a punishment for sin. The identification of theology with culture in this passage is nearly total, and the preservation of these cultural standards in the name of doctrine is sheer archaism.

The presiding elder (3:1-7) is described in terms of rather conventional virtue. The JB does not translate the Greek word *episkopos* as "bishop" here, and all interpreters agree that the word does not designate the type of officer later known as bishop. The presiding elder was probably a member of a committee of elders; this government by elders was the most common type of municipal government in the ancient world, and it survives in the name "alderman" (elder) for a member of the committee which governs a modern city. The early church, it seems, adopted this type of government without any reflection, and scarcely from a belief that Jesus had left explicit instructions for this type of government. The elder should marry only once; this is not a prohibition of polygamy but of a second marriage after the death of the first wife. The early church has an interesting history of the idea that such a marriage showed an incontinence which was less than perfect. The elder should also be a man who will not compromise his fellow Christians in the eyes of unbelievers. In addition, he should manage an orderly household, an obligation which modern clerics are forbidden to meet.

The deacons (3:8-13) had the management of the funds for charitable dispensation. No doubt they also had liturgical functions, but we do not know what they were. The qualities desired are much the same as the qualities for the presiding elder. The "women" (3:11) may be the wives of the deacons or "deaconesses as a distinct office; it cannot be determined which is meant. In either case the women could only assist in the charitable ministries of the church; any liturgical function seems to be forbidden in 2:11-12.

By a digression the author refers to the mystery of the church (3:14-16). The description of the church as that which upholds the truth and keeps it safe (older versions, "the pillar and ground of the truth") illustrates the interest of the author in doctrine. The mystery of the church is Christ, and the proclamation of this mystery in 3:16 is probably from an early liturgical hymn. The closing lines which refer to the proclamation of the pagans and the faith of the world are clearly allusions to the eschatological hope rather than to the historical life of Jesus.

The section on false teachers (4:1-11) begins with the expression of a belief which is found in most apocalyptic sections of the New Testament and in several Jewish apocalyptic works as well. This was the belief that the final age would be preceded by a religious and moral collapse, a kind of last throb of wickedness before it is finally vanquished. The author seems to think he may be witnessing this collapse. Only two errors of the false teachers are mentioned—the prohibition of marriage and of certain foods. This is the earliest mention in the New Testament of the antimarriage heresy, which became more virulent in the second and third centuries. It was common in Gnostic sects; and it should be understood that the prohibition of marriage did not always mean the prohibition of sex. The dietary laws alluded to here do not seem to be the dietary laws of Judaism, although they may have been derived from the Jewish example.

In opposition to these teachers the author states that all creatures are good (thus anticipating the Manichaeism latent in so much of Christian belief and practice). Some ascetic discipline, not specified in its character, is recommended; the author compares it to gymnastic exercise—a real cult in the Hellenistic world not entirely unlike the similar cult in the modern world. The whole doctrinal question is reduced to simple faith in God who wills to save. The "godless myths and old wives' tales" (4:7) cannot be identified.

Timothy is encouraged to do his duty as a minister of the gospel (4:12-16). The allusion to his youth may be a part of the literary fiction of the epistle; in any case Timothy could easily have been much younger than Paul. His work consists in reading aloud (which must mean the Old Testament), preaching (more literally encouragement or exhortation) and teaching (the explanation of the creed). Timothy has a *charisma,* a spiritual gift; this is the same word which is used to describe the gifts at Corinth. But the Corinthian gifts came unbidden when the Spirit willed. The charisma of Timothy is permanent and came to him with the imposition of the hands by which he was ordained to church office. This imposition was done by all the "elders" (not the same word as the "presiding elder" of 3:1). The charisma has now become attached to an office and is conferred by a ritual action.

Some rather pedestrian directions on pastoral practice (5:1-2) recommend that Timothy deal with various groups by sex and age as he would deal with corresponding members of his own family. This is to be done without any compromise of his authority.

In the opinion of many interpreters, the discussion concerning widows (5:3-16) indicates a constituted order of widows, the first such indication of groups within the church. The widows must have pledged themselves in some way to remain within the order; this is suggested by 5:11-12. The widows should be of an age (sixty) which makes a second marriage unlikely; and they must never have contracted a second marriage. We see here again the incipient prejudice against second marriages. Their life is what in modern times is called contemplative (5:5), although the visitation of homes as a charitable work may be suggested by 5:13. Is this order a way of providing for the needs of the widows, who in the ancient world were often among the most helpless? It seems quite probable.

The author seems strangely hostile to younger widows, expecting nothing from them but levity and frivolity. Nothing better can be expected of them, and for their own good and the good of the church they should find another husband.

There is no reason to think that the author has renounced the ideal of Paul in 1 Corinthians 7:40; he is simply realistic, and ready to admit that imperfection is the terminal spiritual state for many members of the church.

The elders (5:17-25) were the committee which governed the local church (Greek *presbuteroi;* see 3:1-7 above). The concern of the writer here is not with their qualities but with the respect due them and the way in which they are to be rebuked for their faults. Since they bear a public responsibility, the rebuke is to be given in public. The caution is given not to ordain any man hastily. This does not imply that Timothy chose the elders, but only that he had to approve the choice. The last two verses (24-25) may refer, rather sententiously, to the difficulty of finding good men; verse 23, the despair of Christian temperance societies for centuries, has to be a digression. It may be remarked that it was probably as dangerous to drink water in the eastern Mediterranean regions then as it is now.

The remarks to slaves prescribe rather unqualified submission (6:1-2); and the author seems to have some awareness of the problems involved in being a Christian slaveowner.

The warning against false teachers (6:3-10) is largely a repetition of the earlier warning. It adds a suggestion that the false teachers were simply moneymakers; but this is an ancient breed in Christianity. The author is somewhat carried away by his thought and delivers a few solemn warnings against avarice. Religion in 6:6 is said to give "self-sufficiency" (Greek *autarkeia*); the use of the word is interesting, for *autarkeia* was a basic virtue which Stoicism guaranteed to its adherents. It is hard to believe that the word is used without deliberate reference to its Stoic background.

The exhortation to Timothy (6:11-16) uses the metaphor of the athletic games, found also in the Pauline letters. A fragment of an early hymn probably appears in 6:15-16. This hymn celebrated Christ's "appearance" (6:14), a word which signified the Second Coming, designated also by the word *parousia,* to which we have referred in earlier epistles. The author warns the rich against their characteristic vice of vanity (6:17-19) and closes with a final warning against false teaching and vain speculation (6:20-21).

The epistle to Titus goes over so much of the same ground as 1 Timothy that comments on the same scale would be merely repetitious. The greeting is much longer and more solemn than the greeting of 1 or 2 Timothy, and it is written in the style of the Pauline greetings. The remarks on elders (Greek *presbuteroi*) are much the same as those made in 1 Timothy 3:1-7. It is clear that these elders have the function of teaching (1:8-9). Neither here nor in 1 Timothy is any liturgical function assigned them.

The false teachers (1:10-16), like the false teachers in 1 Timothy, are described only generally. They also are accused of teaching for gain. But the Jewish influence on the false doctrine is mentioned much more explicitly here. The false doctrine involves "myths" and certain prohibitions, to which the author responds with the adage that to the pure all things are pure. This echoes both the Gospels and Paul (see JB margin).

The instructions to various age groups (2:1-10) are put in rather general terms; indeed they are scarcely specifically Christian. One notices again that the message to wives and slaves is submissive obedience. The warning against such definite bad habits as gossip and drinking among older women and petty thievery among slaves is almost amusing; the author risks being too practical. He stresses the importance of projecting a good image of the Christian community to the unbelieving world.

The basis of Christian moral teaching and life (2:11-15) is the revelation of God's grace in Christ; this imposes a life which is eschatologically oriented—that is, toward the "appearance," the Second Coming. There is hardly any doubt that Jesus Christ is called great God and Savior (2:13); it is a phrase which is found even in the Hellenistic-Roman Caesar cult. It is quite in harmony with later Christology; it is a phrase which Paul would have found difficult to write.

The general instructions (3:1-8) come down rather hard on submissiveness to public authority and politeness to everyone else. This is no doubt a part of the favorable image which the author wished to be projected. He reminds the believers that they were formerly quite different, and that God, our Savior, delivered them out of sheer compassion. The author does not draw the explicit lesson that they should show sheer compassion for others.

The personal message to Titus (3:8-11) is another warning against false doctrine; it is useless speculation and quibbling about genealogies and the Law (1 Timothy 1:3-7). In both letters, the false teachers are not clearly accused of subverting the faith; Paul spoke much more severely of the Judaizers. The personal references (3:12-15), in the hypothesis of a pseudonymous writer, must be a part of his literary fiction.

The "testament," a literary bequest of a famous figure to his sons or disciples, was a common artifice both in Jewish and Hellenistic literature. One need only recall the "Testaments of the Twelve Patriarchs" of the Jewish apocryphal books and the Platonic dialogues *Crito* and *Phaedo*, in which Socrates speaks to his disciples before his execution. If 2 Timothy is pseudonymous, it falls into this class of composition. Thus it is couched in a very personal tone; the author intended to represent Paul's thoughts and feelings on the eve of martyrdom. He did not, however, tell us what he must have known, namely, the time and place in which 2 Timothy should be situated. He rather clearly means to imply Rome.

The greeting and thanksgiving (1:1-5) follow the pattern of the Pauline epistles. Paul opens his exhortation (1:6-18) by recalling Timothy's charismatic gifts of office; we have already touched on this in discussing 1 Timothy 4:14. Paul compares this to his own charisma of the apostolate, which has sustained him in hardship and persecution. The passage has a strong eschatological orientation, and the "appearance," a word characteristic of the pastoral epistles, occurs again (1:10).

The author shows the interest in sound doctrine which we observe in the other pastoral epistles (1:13-14). The reference to particular persons in Ephesus (1:15-18) ought to have a historical basis. We learn that when Paul was imprisoned some people no longer acknowledged his friendship; the names would hardly be mentioned unless they were in some way closer to Paul than others.

Timothy is encouraged to bear up under hardships (2:1-13). He has strength from Christ. His primary mission is to hand on what Paul has taught him; here we see the beginnings of the theme of tradition. The duty of the faithful minister is likened to the duty of the soldier, the athlete and the farmer; all of these are rewarded because they persevere through difficulties. Paul then gives himself as an example; it is the gospel that has put him in prison, but the gospel cannot be imprisoned. A fragment of an early Christian hymn probably appears in 2:11-12. The original reference of the hymn may have been to baptism (see Romans 6:5-11), but the author means to refer it to the apostolic experience of suffering and even of martyrdom.

The author returns to the refutation of false teachers (2:14-26); again we hear of idle and silly speculations. However, he becomes explicit when he mentions the erroneous notion that the resurrection had already occurred (2:18); Hymenaeus is also mentioned in 1 Timothy 1:20. The reference is probably to a Gnostic interpretation of the resurrection; in Gnosticism the material principle is identical with the evil principle, and the resurrection could only be interpreted allegorically as the liberation of the soul from the body. This was probably understood to occur in baptism. The distinction between vessels made for noble purposes and vessels made for base purposes (2:20-21) does not refer to different offices and orders in the church, but to the difference between true teachers and false teachers.

The author speaks of the religious and moral collapse of the eschatological period (3:1-5). We have mentioned this theme in 1 Timothy 4:1. In particular, this period will suffer from false teachers (3:6-9). The misogyny of the author is apparent in the way in which he speaks of the weakness that women exhibit for spiritual charlatans. Jannes and Jambres (3:8) were names which Jewish tradition gave to the Egyptian magicians who attempted to match the miraculous powers of Moses (Exodus 7:8-13). The author again exhorts Timothy to perseverance in persecution, and reveals his conviction that it is inevitable for the Christian. This conviction does not appear in the Pauline epistles; Christians of the first generation apparently did not forsee the hostility which the gospel would elicit both in popular feelings and in the officials of the Roman government. The references to Paul's persecutions are well chosen for Timothy; they are the persecutions which occurred in Lystra, Timothy's native city, and the neighboring cities of Antioch (in Pisidia) and Iconium.

The author again exhorts to fidelity to sound doctrine (3:14-17). To sound doctrine is added a knowledge of the scriptures, by which the author must mean the books of the Old Testament; at his time, as far as we know, no Christian writing would be placed on the same level. This is the first occurrence in Christian literature of the word "inspired" being applied to the scriptures; later theology of inspiration has its origin in this passage.

The charge to Timothy (4:1-9) is attributed to Paul as his final saying—his "testament." It is put with all solemnity, with the invocation of God and Jesus Christ, and with reference to the eschatological judgment at the "appearance," the word already noted in the pastoral epistles. Timothy must proclaim the word without ceasing; there is no time when proclamation is unsuitable. Again the author insists on sound doctrine. In the last days they will be deceived by "myths," the aberration which the author has already mentioned several times. Against these Timothy is to be brave and unyielding, clinging to the gospel. The author does not promise Timothy the martyrdom which Paul experienced. The martyrdom of Paul is a libation, the offering of wine which accompanied meat and cereal offerings both in Judaism and in paganism. Paul describes his own life in terms of the athletic games. We have noticed that this imagery is common enough in the epistles, almost as common as the imagery of athletic competition is in modern speech. The crown (laurel, olive or pine) was awarded to victors in the games (1 Corinthians 9:25). The "day" is the day of the "appearance"—the *parousia.*

The personal greetings and conclusion (4:9-22) seem to be quite elaborate for a literary fiction, and those who believe that the letter contains fragments from Paul himself look for them in this passage. But no certain conclusions can be established. The names are all (except the Roman Christians in 4:21) known in Acts and the Pauline epistles.

The cloak (4:13), the outer garment necessary in the Mediterranean winter months, must have been missing so long (in any hypothesis) that Paul would have had to purchase or borrow another one. The request for the scrolls shows what the apostle and evangelist had to carry in their baggage. The "defense" (4:16), literally "first defense," may allude to the technical legal Latin phrase *prima actio,* the preliminary investigation. As in 1:15, there is a complaint that Paul has been forsaken by some followers.

Epistle to Philemon

This is the only personal letter of Paul in the entire collection; and no scholar doubts its genuinity. Philemon was a Christian of Colossae (so it is generally thought); he was probably a man of means, since the church met in his house and he was a slaveowner. Paul wrote from prison, and here the imprisonment is probably that mentioned in Acts 28. We have already mentioned that Colossians and Philemon may have been sent in the same dispatch. The greetings and thanksgiving are like the letters of Paul to churches; but they do preface the request for a favor.

Onesimus was a fugitive slave who had run away from the household of Philemon. He had probably stolen something for the escape (v. 18). He drifted to Rome, where he met Paul and was converted to Christianity. Paul probably did not learn at once that he was a fugitive slave. When he learned it, he sent Onesimus back and wrote this letter. He does not clearly ask Philemon to set Onesimus free, but to receive him as a brother—that is, as a fellow Christian; more than that, he asks Philemon to receive him as one especially dear to Paul.

Paul offers to pay for any loss Philemon has incurred; and —not without a certain deviousness—Paul asks Philemon to put him up when he arrives, which he expects will be soon. Philemon could hardly have done this favor if he had to report to Paul that Onesimus had received the punishment which a fugitive slave deserved. Slavery in Roman law was chattel slavery. The master could punish the offending slave as he wished; and short of murder or rape of the owner's wife or daughter, flight was the worst offense a slave could commit. Within the law and with no social stigma Philemon could have had Onesimus killed, tortured, mutilated, scourged or—the lightest punishment—branded with a hot iron. This is the background of Paul's "small favor." He really asks no more of Philemon than forgiveness; it is not clear, as we have said, that he asks Philemon to free his slave. The modern reader does not know what a surprise such a request would have been to a Roman slaveowner. Paul does hint that he would like to have Onesimus returned to him—not liberated, but made a gift to Paul.

The modern reader is often indignant that Paul returned a fugitive slave, even with such a letter. The abolitionist would have turned him loose; and the abolitionist is offended because Paul was not an abolitionist. Paul responds to this in verse 14; the act of kindness which is forced is really not an act of kindness. Unlike the abolitionist, Paul thinks of Philemon as well as of Onesimus; genuine Christianity demands a renunciation from both. How did Paul persuade Onesimus to return? No one thinks that he did it by threatening to turn Onesimus in to the police. Slaveowning societies do not treat fugitive slaves as Paul asked Philemon to treat Onesimus. There is a tradition that Paul's maneuver was successful, and that the Onesimus mentioned as bishop of Ephesus by Ignatius of Antioch was the former slave. Whatever the outcome, Paul settled the question by putting a Christian decision before each of the parties involved. He did not need to attack the institution of slavery to solve this particular problem, nor would the problem have been solved by such an attack.

\+ + +

THE SOCIAL SILENCE OF THE NEW TESTAMENT

Slavery is not the only problem on which many modern readers have judged the New Testament unsatisfactory. The New Testament is silent on politics; Rome is barely mentioned and never criticized. Jesus' saying, "Render to Caesar what belongs to Caesar," was uttered in the reign of Tiberius. Would he have said anything different in the reign of Tiberius' successor, Caligula, who could be judged criminally insane by any standard? The New Testament has no recommendations for improving the political structure.

We have adverted to bits of misogyny scattered through the epistles. We have said that these sayings are culturally conditioned. Is there no concern in the New Testament for the full rights of women as human beings? In a world in which the war on poverty has become a slogan, sayings like "Blessed are you, you poor people" and "Sell what you have and give to the poor" seem feeble. Now we have what appears to be a tacit acceptance of chattel slavery. For those who wish to reform social institutions the New Testament seems to have nothing to say.

In fact it does not say anything, and there is little honesty or sense in pretending that it does. The thrust of the New Testament is toward the reformation of the individual person, a reformation which is not accomplished by law and order but by the free decision of the individual person.

It is not a question of changing the institutions through changing the persons; changing the individual person by leading the person to his fulfillment is an end which needs no further end to justify itself. Neither Paul nor Jesus said a word against the institution of slavery, as they said no revolutionary word against the Roman Empire—a silence which did not endear Jesus to those of his fellow Jews called Zealots. Yet both Jesus and Paul proved, as well as any modern radicals have done, that the state could not coerce them to do evil. Paul simply proposed an ethic which, fully understood, made it impossible for one man to own another. Only by the Christian ethic has any society ever abolished slavery. As Paul said to Philemon, if it is force, it is not kindness; and we do wish to foster kindness, not merely to bridle cruelty. As long as it is only bridled, we remain in a cruel world. Similarly, poverty will endure as long as men allow their competitive and dominative instincts to rule over compassion. The institutions can be improved, but if men are not, are the institutions really improved?

This should not be taken to imply that the New Testament or Christians are indifferent to social institutions or uninterested in their improvement. I have spoken of the New Testament thrust toward the individual; this thrust is not so unworldly that the Christian cares nothing about his society. Insofar as society is people, it would be un-Christian not to protest against the cruelty of man to man, and not to seek to alter the institutions which foster cruelty. My point about slavery and poverty is that the New Testament seeks the most profound alteration of institutions which is possible. The modern radical is unhappy because the Christian thrust seems so slow. Perhaps the modern radical has something to learn about the demonic in man. When social action is proposed, the New Testament does not discourage it; it simply moves in a different way. It was written in a world which knew no social action, and its novelty was not in the creation of social action but in another type of action. It can hardly be said that it has been tried and failed. We do not yet know that social action will move against the demons any more swiftly. At the risk of being tediously repetitious, I must state that when we protect ourselves against our fellow man we have not changed him. And we should have learned that the price of such protection has often been that we become that against which we protect ourselves. The Christian may have to protect himself against his fellow man by dying for him; and he cannot do this unless he knows that the fellow man and himself are one.

The New Testament is culturally conditioned as far as social action is concerned. The student of the New Testament recognizes that social action, like electricity, is the product of modern technology. He will use it with a recognition of its dangers and of the limits of its achievement. One clear limit is that it will not bring to pass the reign of God.

Chapter Eleven
EPISTLE TO THE HEBREWS

The epistle to the Hebrews is not attributed to Paul anywhere within its contents, and it does not even pretend to be an epistle; it lacks the epistolary greeting. The conclusion (13:20-25) does indeed suit an epistle, but this could easily have been added as a literary fiction to attribute the work to Paul. Nor is there any allusion within the epistle to the people addressed, as is usual in the letters of Paul. It is generally regarded as a homily, not written as an epistle, although it may have been distributed to several churches.

If the criteria of style, vocabulary and thought are ever valid, they are here convincing that the epistle was neither written by Paul nor commissioned by him. This is a different world of speech and thought from the epistles of Paul. Even in the early church the attribution to Paul does not appear before the late second century. Naturally, other well-known persons of the apostolic church have been suggested; the most interesting possibilities are Barnabas and Apollos. The author shows certain traits of what is called Alexandrian thought (so called from the city of Alexandria, perhaps the most active intellectual center of the Roman Empire at the time the epistle was written). These traits are well illustrated in the writings of Philo of Alexandria, a Jewish scholar nearly contemporary with Jesus. The author of this epistle does not show the influence of Philo, but he writes like a man from the same intellectual circle. Paul himself nowhere shows the Alexandrian influence.

Since the author is unknown, the date is uncertain. It is evident from the content, however, that much of the author's thesis could have been supported by the destruction of the temple of Jerusalem and the abolition of Jewish sacrificial ritual in A.D. 70. We cannot assume that the author had to use this if it were available, but the fact that he did not use it suggests an earlier date.

The title "to the Hebrews" is not attested before the third century; but there is hardly any manuscript evidence for anything before this date. The contents would certainly be easier for Jewish Christians than for Gentiles; the epistle is loaded with allusions to Jewish ritual worship. The author obviously seems to be a Jewish Christian, and he appears to be speaking to some threat of apostasy not specified. It is not without interest that a homily written by a Jewish Christian for Jewish Christians is one of the better examples of Greek style in the New Testament. The epistle displays nothing of the Judaizing against which Paul wrote in most of the other letters.

The prologue (1:1-4) contrasts the sacred revelation of the books of the Old Testament with the fullness of the revelation of the Son. To the Jews, the very opening sentence is militant. The Christology of the prologue is what we have called "advanced." The author comes as close to the later formula of unity of nature as it was possible without the philosophical language; he wishes to preserve the distinction between Father and Son without making the Son an inferior being. Like Paul, he sees the fullness of the glory of the Son as hidden before the exaltation of the Son. But the Son is the agent of creation; he is not only pre-existent, but prior to creation.

The superiority of the Son to the angels is shown in a series of seven Old Testament texts, employed according to Alexandrian rabbinical learning. In fact none of the texts speak of the Son; they refer to God himself or to the messianic king. They show sonship, the right to worship, eternal kingship, eternity and creative power, and exaltation to equality with God (the right hand). Why the controversy with the angels? We have had occasion to refer to the interest of later Judaism in angels and the speculations about their ranks and works. To Jews the proclamation of Jesus as a pre-existent Messiah could easily be understood to signify that he was one of the angels—perhaps supreme in dignity, but nevertheless one of a number of intermediate beings. The author insists on his unique nature and position.

We have remarked that the author seems to address himself to the danger of apostasy; this appears in his exhortation to fidelity (2:1-4). The gospel is contrasted with the Law, brought through the mediation of angels (see Galatians 3:19); the gospel is superior just through the excellence of its mediator. Yet the Law carried within itself penalties, but the author is sure that the offender cannot escape. The proclaimer is the Lord (by which he means Jesus), and the gospel is attested by miraculous signs and wonders; in this also the gospel excels the Law, which was attested by the signs and wonders upon Pharaoh.

The author returns to the theme of the superiority of Christ to the angels (2:5-18). He adduces Psalm 8:4-6 for this purpose; but he can use this text only because the Greek Old Testament gives him the key words "for a short while," which is an inaccurate rendition of the Hebrew. "Son of man" is understood to refer to Jesus, but the original text has no such reference. So the text is interpreted to speak of the temporary humiliation of Christ in his incarnation, and of the universal cosmic dominion which is granted him in his exaltation. The author adds that it was necessary for Christ to experience death, and this leads him into his next development. The one who leads the children (of God) to glory must be of the same stock as they are. This necessity arises from his priesthood, the theme which the writer reaches at the close of this paragraph. The priest who represents a group before God must be a member of the group; no foreigner or stranger is acceptable. This, of course, demands that he share their flesh and blood, and also that he share flesh and blood in the condition in which they share it. Flesh and blood are the condition of moral weakness and mortality. Christ has suffered and died; he has also experienced temptation, and thus he knows the condition of sinful flesh without having sinned himself. Later theology has often rebelled at the full implications of this statement. The statement does not imply that the author knew the Gospel account of the temptation of Jesus (Mark 1:12-13; Matthew 4:1-11; Luke 4:1-13). The theme is that Jesus shared the human experience completely, and this is found in a document with advanced Christology. The experience enabled hirn not only to be the agent of salvation but to have compassion (2:17; see 5:1-2) and to become perfect (2:10). This last phrase refers to his role as leader of salvation.

Christ is superior not only to the angels, but to Moses (3:1-6). This theme, together with the exhortation that the readers should turn their eyes to Jesus, seems to be addressed to Jewish rather than to Gentile Christians. One may compare this with 2 Corinthians 3:4-18; the author seems to derive nothing from 2 Corinthians, although his argument is equally involved. The "house" is the ancient Israel whose legitimate continuation is the new Israel of the church. The builder is God; he is not Moses or Christ. The dignity of Christ is greater because he is the son in the house; Moses was faithful, but as a servant. The text is similar to the image of the slave and the son in Galatians 4:1-7.

The author turns to the theme of "the Rest," the goal of the forty years' wandering of the exodus, denied to the unbelieving Israelites according to Psalm 95:7-11. The Rest is really identical with the Promised Land; but the author chooses the theme of the Rest because it merits him to play with the theme of the eternal Sabbath rest of God after six days of creation (4:5, 10; Genesis 2:2). The rest promised to Israel is taken as a type of the Rest granted the believers through the saving work of Christ. Ancient Israel certainly attained no permanent rest, as history had proved. The reason why they had not attained it was lack of faith, the defect which prevented their ancestors from achieving the Rest. According to the narrative of the book of Numbers, all the adult Israelites who disbelieved the report of Joshua and Caleb regarding the Promised Land were punished by death in the dessert and denial of entrance to the Promised Land. Lack of faith in the Messiah prevents their descendents from entering into the Rest to which Christ leads them. This is the eternal Rest, initiated by the rest of God after his creative work. Obviously, this is more than a primitive form of Zionism; the type will not be fulfilled by the establishment of the people of God in Palestine. The eternal Rest is eschatological, although the epistle is not a strongly eschatological composition.

The saying about the word of God (4:12-13) is somewhat unrelated to the context. The word of God does not mean simply the scriptures, nor, at the other extreme, is it identified with the person of Jesus; this Johannine idiom is not found elsewhere in the New Testament. Nor is it just the gospel proclaimed by Jesus and the apostles. More generally than any of these, it is any and all communication from God, whether through scripture or prophets or apostles. The point is that it is speech which compels an answer and makes evasion impossible. One can disbelieve, but one cannot pretend that one believes or that one never heard the word. In this sense it is a word of judgment.

The theme of the compassionate high priest (4:14-5:10) has already been sketched out in 2:10-18. Jesus knows compassion because he knows temptation; and the author knows no temptation which is excluded, although it is doubtful that he meant to be as explicit as he sounds. For instance, what would have been his answer if he had been asked whether he meant to include temptations of the flesh, the one temptation which theology and devotion have consistently refused to permit? Would he have said that the absence of such temptation would have made Jesus less aware of our weakness and therefore less compassionate? The author may not have felt the Manichean and Jansenist repugnance to temptations of the flesh which is the most common Roman Catholic attitude. In any case, the difference he proposes between Jesus and other men is not that Jesus was not tempted, but that Jesus did not sin. For many believers this has not been enough of a difference.

Jesus is contrasted with the Jewish high priest. Like him, he is a man taken from among men; we have noticed that the priest must be a member of the group for whom he mediates. The author has already made the point that compassion in

Jesus is based on a consciousness of common weakness, but now he is careful to avoid the implication that this could mean a common sinfulness; Jesus does not have to offer sacrifice on his own behalf. The only ritual action in which the high priest atoned for himself was the ritual of the Day of Atonement (Leviticus 16:6). The reference to sinners as "the ignorant and the uncertain" probably alludes to the sin-offering and the guilt-offering, sacrifices offered under the Levitical law for sins committed in error or ignorance. There was no ritual offering for sins committed "with a high hand," with fully deliberate malice (Numbers 15:30). Even this venial weakness did not lead Jesus into sin.

Jesus, like the Jewish high priest, had to be constituted as priest by God, not merely by human appointment. This appointment is verified by the texts from Psalms 2:7 (originally referred to the Davidic king) and 110:4 (also referred to the Davidic king in his role as priest-king). Jesus did indeed pray for himself, but only for deliverance from death. His prayer was heard only in the resurrection. In submitting to death, from which he rose, he became perfect as Messiah-Savior. Learning to obey through suffering does not imply the medicinal value which suffering has for sinners; it means that he shared the experience of medicinal suffering, even though he did not need it. He is fully in communion with those whom he saves, fully acquainted with the human condition.

The author now embarks on the major topic of his homily, the high priesthood of Christ. He opens his treatment with a mild rebuke of his listeners. It is impossible to be specific about the fault he found in them. The figure of milk, the food of infants, rather than the solid food of adults, is used in 1 Corinthians 3:2. In that passage, as in this one, the figure cuts sharply; both writers tell the listeners that they have not yet grown up. The figure here is even sharper: The author says with unconcealed sarcasm that his listeners should be far enough advanced to be teachers of others. This does not surely imply that they have any office in the Christian community, nor, as a few interpreters have suggested, that they were Jewish priests who had become Christians.

In spite of the sarcasm about the ignorance of his listeners, the author proceeds to tell them that he will not go over elementary instruction, but will proceed to the exposition of his topic, which is the high priesthood of Christ (6:1-8). The six topics mentioned (6:1-2) raise no particular questions, except the "baptism"; these are thought by commentators not to mean the sacrament of initiation, but ritual ablutions, common in Judaism and probably retained by Jewish Christians. To this he adds some remarks about the impossibility of repentance for those who have been baptized and have apostatized. "Illuminated" (6:4) is a common term in early Christian literature for the baptized. To this the author adds the gifts of the Holy Spirit, which may mean the charismatic gifts such as those mentioned in 1 Corinthians.

Theologians are never more uneasy than they are when a biblical writer says something which appears to be in flat contradiction with an accepted doctrine. The church has taught, almost from the beginning, that there is no sin which cannot be forgiven. But there was opposition to this generous forgiveness in the early church. Tertullian is an example of those who taught that some sins admit no forgiveness; and among the three he mentioned was apostasy, the sin mentioned here. He would agree with the author that apostasy is a re-enactment of the crucifixion of Christ. The other two unforgivable sins were murder and adultery. He did not mean merely that there was no sacramental reconciliation with the church for these sins, but that man could commit sins which put him out of reach of the mercy of God. The church did not accept his rigor, as it has never accepted similar rigorous views. But the church has been uncomfortable with the author of the epistle to the Hebrews.

Theologians have generally said that the author, who does not speak with the technical precision of later theologians, speaks of "impossibility" in the sense of improbability. No New Testament writer spoke with the precision of later theologians. If Paul had had a course in modern dogmatic theology, he could never have said some of the things which he did say about the Trinity and the Incarnation. It has rarely occurred to the fathers of ecumenical councils and to theologians that they may have sought a precision of language which could distort the truths in which they believed. Equivalently, they reconcile themselves with the author of the epistle to the Hebrews by granting him a freedom of speech which they deny themselves.

As a practical pastoral principle it is true that apostasy takes away the principle on which repentance is founded. While the author did not distinguish between impossibility and improbability, we may do so; and it does not follow from his statement that he would refuse to receive penitent apostates, but that he would not expect them to appear. It is not characteristic of the New Testament to place limits on God's forgiveness; it does occur to the writers, as it occurs to us, to place limits on the capacity of man to seek forgiveness. It cannot be denied that the text illustrates a rigor which in later Christianity has often assumed very disagreeable forms, to put it mildly. The Christian normally, like the author of the epistle, looks at the apostate as the American looks at Benedict Arnold. We are not sure that we can transfer our attitude to God.

We noticed that the author of the epistle is not afraid to use sarcasm with his listeners (5:11-14) and to warn them of the danger of apostasy in terms so severe that his language is open to an intolerably rigid interpretation. Now he shifts to a more encouraging tone in his exhortation (6:9-12). The reason for the change to a more encouraging tone is the charity of those to whom he speaks; this is the fundamental Christian virtue, and if they have charity they have what is most necessary. The quality of their charity permits the author to express some assurances that they will persevere.

He leads into the theme of the priesthood of Jesus, which he certainly introduces at great length, by a discussion of the oath of God (6:13-20). The history of salvation begins with the oath of God to Abraham (Genesis 22:16). The oath is the supreme effort of man to be truthful—here not of what is affirmed but of what is promised. God makes the same supreme effort, although his promise needs no asseveration. The truthfulness of man is supported by the invocation of the deity; the truthfulness of God can be supported only by the invocation of himself. God has done this for Abraham; and since the oath was a promise of numerous progeny, the author doubtless sees its fulfillment in the church. This same divine power and truthfulness has constituted Jesus the high priest.

The exposition of the priesthood of Christ begins (7:1-28) with a midrashic interpretation of Genesis 14:18-20. Those who find it hard to understand what interpreters mean by midrash can perhaps learn more easily by studying this example than by trying to work through abstract definitions. This passage in Genesis and Psalm 110:4 are the only passages of the Old Testament where Melchizedek is mentioned. Presupposed to the interpretation is the unproved assumption that Melchizedek is a type of Christ. The assumption is somewhat helped by the fact that Melchizedek has nothing to do with any Israelite institution and by certain resemblances between Melchizedek and Christ which can be detected by rabbinical interpretation; these will be mentioned shortly. Melchizedek was priest-king of Salem, which means Jerusalem. The Canaanite king was normally also the high priest of the city-state, and Psalm 110:4 accords the same dignity to David; but this dual role did not endure in the Jerusalem monarchy. The author plays both on the name of Melchizedek ("righteous king," originally "My king is Zedek [a divine name]") and Salem (Hebrew *shalom*, "peace," originally Shalem [a divine name]). These are the first two resemblances between Melchizedek and Christ. His ancestry is not mentioned; on the rabbinical principle that what is not mentioned in Holy Writ does not exist, he is likened to Christ, who has no human genealogy.

The author then argues that Melchizedek was a person of greater dignity than Abraham. Abraham gave Melchizedek a tenth of the booty of the battle; the reasons for this are not stated, and it appears to be a gift in token of services not stated. The author sees in this the tithes which the Israelites owed the Levitical priesthood; these were not a gift, but the fulfillment of a duty. On the rabbinical principle that the descendant was present "in the loins" of his ancestor, Levi, the ancestor of the priesthood, paid tithes to Melchizedek and thus acknowledged the superiority of his priesthood. Furthermore, Levi (in Abraham) was blessed by Melchizedek; and the author states a principle that a blessing is given by the superior to the inferior, a principle which is not in harmony with the Old Testament idea of blessing.

The author then argues simply that if the Levitical priesthood had been perfect, God would not have instituted a new priesthood—which might appear to a Jewish reader as begging the question (7:11-14). But the author is using exactly the type of midrashic exegesis which the Jewish reader would find it difficult to contest. It is clearly new because Christ, the new high priest, is not from the priestly tribe of Levi but from the tribe of Judah—the royal tribe, but the author is not interested in pushing this theme. Nor is the author concerned with the fact that the Judahite ancestry of Jesus does not fit perfectly with 7:3. His point is an entirely new priesthood and—what he elaborates later—the abrogation of the old priesthood. The "perfection" (7:11,18) which is lacking in the Levitical priesthood is probably the ministry of the reconciliation of sinners with God. Only Jesus is the perfect agent of this reconciliation; the Levitical ritual did not achieve it. The argument is parallel to the argument of Paul in Romans about the Law; but Paul pays little attention to the ritual of atonement.

Still another reason for the superiority of the priesthood of Christ is seen in the eternity of his priesthood (7:15-25). This is based on the eternal life which is his by virtue of his resurrection. The eternity of his priesthood is stated in the text of Psalm 110:4 about Melchizedek; David is a priest forever "according to the order of Melchizedek." The midrashic quality of this interpretation scarcely needs comment; but the author goes on to see in this declaration an implicit abolition of the Levitical priesthood. Actually his charge is that the Levitical priesthood fell short of perfection; as we have seen, this means that it did not effectively take away sin.

The author returns to the oath of God as an assurance of the effective and eternal priesthood of Christ, a theme already used in reference to Abraham (6:13-20). The eternity of the priesthood is shown in the fact that Christ has risen to live forever; the Levitical priesthood, on the contrary, was vested in mortal men.

The author summarizes the contrast (7:26-28). We have seen that the priest must be one of the group which he represents; but the author affirms that he should not share entirely the group's needs. He should not have to offer sacrifices for his own sins before he can offer atonement for the sins of others. He probably would not think of this were he not proposing Jesus as the ideal high priest; yet, in fact, priestly ritual all over the world has demanded that priests achieve at least a ritual purity before they minister on behalf of those in whom this ritual purity is not required. The Levitical law did not in fact require, as the author seems to imply, that the high priest should offer sacrifice daily in atonement for his own sins. Interpreters generally think that here the author's memory failed him.

The author now turns to the superiority of the place of offering (8:1-5). The Levitical priesthood offered sacrifice in the tabernacle; commentators have noticed that the author never refers to the temple of Jerusalem. This silence almost surely has implications about the attitude of the author toward this temple, but he never makes it explicit. The priesthood of Christ is exercised in heaven where he is enthroned at the right hand of God; this is based on Psalm 110:1. Implicit here is a mythological belief that earthly reality is a counterpart of the heavenly and higher reality. This belief was known in the ancient Near East, in which the earthly temple was the imitation of the heavenly palace of the god. It appears less emphatically in the Old Testament; Moses is shown a model of the heavenly tabernacle according to which the earthly tabernacle is to be built (Exodus 25:9). That the visible reality is an imitation of the spiritual reality is also a theme of Platonism, and it is found in Philo of Alexandria. The superiority of Christ is also seen in the quality of his offerings, which the author introduces later. But the author states that the superior quality of his offering would exclude him from the Levitical priesthood, which deals only in the imitations of the heavenly reality.

Christ is also the mediator of the new covenant (8:6-12). By an argument already used, the author says that if the old covenant had been perfect God would not have instituted a new one. But here he is not begging the question, and he quotes the entire passage of Jeremiah in which a new covenant is promised. In fact the text is not entirely relevant to his purpose, since it is not concerned with sacrificial ritual at all. It is concerned with the Law, which will be revealed in the heart of each man and not externally on written tablets. The text is much more relevant to Paul's statements on the abrogation of the Law; strangely Paul does not make use of this text.

The excellence of the priesthood is now shown by a contrast with the sacrificial ritual of the Levitical priesthood. The ritual of the Levitical priesthood is set forth in some detail although with nothing like the fullness of the book of Leviticus. The author describes the two parts of the tabernacle, the Holy Place and the Most Holy Place (the "Holy of Holies"). The latter was an inner chamber, separated from the Holy Place by a curtain—the curtain rent in the midrash of Matthew 27:51. Only the priests were allowed to enter the Holy Place, and then only on clearly defined ritual occasions. The author adds to the ambiguity of the biblical sources concerning the contents of the ark of the covenant; this is not the place to discuss this problem, which in any case cannot be settled; we can apply to ourselves the statement of the author in 9:5.

The Most Holy Place, on the other hand, was accessible only to the high priest during the ritual of the Day of Atonement (Leviticus 16). The author repeats his theme that the high priest had to offer an atoning sacrifice frist for his own sins and then for the sins of the people; this was indeed a part of the ritual of the Day of Atonement, but it did not occur elsewhere in the ritual. The author then draws conclusions about the effectiveness of this ritual. It dealt only with the externals and did not really reconcile man to God, nor did it take away sin. More than that, the author deduces from the two chambers, the Holy Place and the Most Holy Place, the conclusion that the Levitical ritual denied the community any access to God. This he will contrast with the priesthood of Christ, the mediator who makes God accessible to all who believe in him.

In contrast, the priestly offering of Christ has none of the limitations of the Levitical ritual (9:11-28). In the first place, Christ enters the heavenly Holy Place, not merely the earthly tabernacle, the imitation of the heavenly tabernacle. In the second place, he offers his own blood rather than the blood of animals. Outside of the formulae of the Eucharist in the Synoptic Gospels and in Paul, this is the earliest mention of the blood of Jesus as a sacrificial offering. The author expands in the following verses the atoning function of the blood in sacrifice. In fact this opens a question too complex to be treated here; for the blood was of great importance in the Israelite sacrificial ritual, perhaps more important than the author knew; it appears that he did not fully understand the complex symbolism of the ritual of the blood. But the effectiveness of the blood of Christ is stated in 9:14; no such claim was ever made for the blood of the sacrificial animals in the Levitical ritual of sacrifice.

The author now returns to the theme of the new covenant; but his argument becomes extremely complicated. The Greek word *diatheke*—by which the Greek Bible renders the Hebrew word *berit*, covenant—also means last will and testament. The author deliberately plays upon this double meaning of the Greek word (which it would not have for Greeks who were unacquainted with the Greek translation of the Old Testament). He argues that a will (covenant) has no effect until the testator has died. Thus the death of Christ, the testator, is necessary in order that the new covenant (will) should become effective. This is surely as close to a merely verbal argument as any biblical writer ever comes. Yet what appears to us a merely verbal argument was esteemed in the rabbinical circles which the author echoes; and if he was writing for Jewish Christians, this was the kind of exposition which would most surely reach them.

The author concludes from the necessity of the death of the testator that even the first covenant of Moses needed a death in order that it might become valid. The need was met by the death of sacrificial animals. Death alone, however, was insufficient for the purpose; the ritual of the sprinkling of the blood was also necessary. Here the author pushes his verbal argument to the limit. Death was necessary for the validity of a *diatheke* (will and testament); the sprinkling of the blood was necessary for the validity of a *diatheke* (covenant). It is impossible to reproduce this argument in English. It is impossible to show the modern reader that such an argument was meant seriously and was taken seriously. Every word of the Scripture had a fullness of meaning. The Scripture was not understood until this fullness of meaning was exhausted. The principle was taught and practiced by the rabbis. Christian rabbis by a disagreeable application of this principle asserted that the fullness of meaning was not understood unless one admitted that the Scripture always spoke of the Messiah (the Christ).

The author is willing to accept the Levitical principle that the ritual of the blood is necessary in any ritual atonement (9:22). But when he introduces the theme of the sprinkling of blood as the rite of purifying the sanctuary, he involves himself in difficulties; for how can the heavenly sanctuary be purified? Actually he never says that Christ purified the heavenly sanctuary; and thus, by more than usual indirection, he again makes his point of the excellence of the sacrifice of Christ.

His final point in this section involves both himself and his interpreters in difficulty. The sacrifice of Christ is superior to the Levitical sacrifices not only for the reasons alleged, but also because it had to be offered only once. A perfect sacrifice cannot be repeated. He compares this one sacrifice to the one death of the human person. Man dies once and then judgment; Christ dies once and then forgiveness. The difficulty this statement raises with the ritual of the Roman Catholic Mass is ancient and celebrated, and it was exploited by the early Reformers. Roman Catholics have responded in various ways, not all of them consistent with each other. But in order to retain the epistle to the Hebrews within the compass of Roman Catholic belief, they have been compelled to say that the Mass is not a new sacrifice in addition to the sacrifice of Christ. It is the one sacrifice of Christ, perfect and incapable of repetition, which gives validity to the Mass, which must in some way be identified with the one sacrifice of Christ. Roman Catholic theology has never reached a consensus on how the unity of the sacrifice of Christ and the multiplicity of the sacrifice of the Mass are to be reconciled. But it admits that the problem has to be explained some way; and it insists that the same apostolic church which produced the epistle to the Hebrews also gave the church the precept of repeating the Eucharistic rite. It is not without interest that the author of the epistle never mentions the Eucharistic rite.

A further question, not associated with the controversies of the Reformation, has to do with the consistency of the author with himself. Was the sacrifice of Christ completed with the cross, or was it completed only with his entrance into the heavenly sanctuary? The author's belief in the earthly counterpart of the heavenly reality does indeed suggest that the priesthood of Christ could be fulfilled only in his exaltation. Here his priesthood became eternal and his sacrifice an offering of eternal validity. Yet this view would be inconsistent not only with the general New Testament view of the efficacy of the atoning death, but even with the author's own theology. That something was lacking in the death of Christ was a view which the New Testament authors found intolerable.

And this is a sufficient reason to conclude that the author of the epistle did not express this view. On the other hand, it must be conceded that his desire to describe the saving act of God in Christ in terms of the Levitical ritual of sacrifice led him further than he intended to go. If we pursue his argument with rigorous allegory, we may drive him further than he wished to go not only in this detail but in others. It is simpler and more honest to grant that the author did not see the full extent to which his argument might be pushed. Had he seen it, he might have restated his thesis. But he would never have questioned nor allowed others to question his basic contention that the saving act of God in Christ superseded all the atoning ritual of the Levitical code. He would insist that however it is to be phrased, this saving act moved against sin and achieved a reconciliation of man with God which the Levitical ritual never achieved nor claimed to achieve. And the modern reader may conclude that one who embarks on rabbinical and midrashic interpretation should not be surprised at any trouble which he encounters.

The author now argues the inefficacy of the Levitical sacrifices (10:1-18). He first contrasts the "shadow" with the "reality"; these words, like the JB translation, render a phrase which it is difficult to render literally into English. Commentators think that the author is not referring to the heavenly-earthly contrast mentioned above (8:1-5). But the author has already called the sacrifice of Christ the perfect heavenly sacrifice; and there seems to be no need for this precision. The inefficacy of the sacrifices is deduced from their repetition. The author does not advert to the problem which new sins create; but it has to be admitted, in view of his belief that apostasy is not forgiven, that he may have been somewhat rigorous in his attitude toward other sins committed after baptism. The author also quotes Psalm 40:6-8, which is not perfectly relevant. The text says that obedience is better than sacrifice, a fairly common theme in the books of the prophets. It does not compare inferior sacrifices with better sacrifices. But the author affirms that the obedience of Jesus was accomplished by a sacrificial act (10:10). The "recalling of sins" (10:3) is an obscure phrase. It can mean the ritual confession of past sins; but it can also mean that the offering of sacrifice for sins recalls them to God's memory and thus risks exciting his anger.

The daily ritual performance of the Levitical priests is contrasted with the enthronement of Christ; and possibly the author means to contrast sitting, the posture of dignity and repose, with standing, the posture of service and submission. Christ can sit enthroned because his priestly ministry is finished. The "perfection" of the consecrated may be noticed (10:14); the idea fits the pattern of rigor suggested above. The author quotes again the new covenant passage of Jeremiah 31:31-34, but with a different interest. He uses it here because of the statement that God will no longer recall sins in the new covenant. This supports his thesis that the perfect sacrifice of Christ completely destroys sin and its remembrance.

The author now turns to the topic of faith, which is the main topic in 10:19—12:29. From 10:19 to 10:39 the author gives a lengthy introduction to the topic. He contrasts the veil of the tabernacle, which shut off men from access to God, with the blood of Jesus, which opens the way to God. By a quaint conceit he likens the "flesh" of Jesus to the veil. The word "flesh" is deliberately chosen rather than "body." He would agree with Paul (1 Corinthians 15:50) that flesh and blood cannot inherit the kingdom of God. Flesh, we have noticed, means man in his moral weakness and mortality. It is the body of Jesus that rises, not his flesh. The entrance is accomplished by baptism (10:22), and the innocence of baptism will be preserved through hope and charity. Love is fostered in "the meetings of the assembly," for which the author employs a word used nowhere else in the New Testament. One almost wonders whether the author is deliberately seeking a word with no Eucharistic implications.

The author seems to say in 10:26 what has been hinted in some preceding passages, that there is no atonement for any sin committed after baptism; and in this sense certainly the sacrifice of Christ would be once and for all perfect. The rigor of the author finds expression in 10:26-31; he piles up Scripture texts which threaten punishment for sin and applies them to the believer who relapses. Interpreters suggest that the language is less rigorous than it seems and that only the sin of apostasy is meant; but the language more obviously signifies that the author believes that any deliberate and serious sin after baptism is a form of apostasy.

Against this danger the author finds reason for encouragement (10:32-39). He speaks to those who have already persevered through persecution. He mentions insults, violence and imprisonment, but he does not mention death, and death for the faith could scarcely have become so casual that it could be left out of such an enumeration. Since they have gone so far, there is good assurance that they can continue. But to persevere they will need faith, and he quotes Habakkuk 2:3-4. "The one that is coming" he interprets as Christ in the Parousia; in Habakkuk, however, it is not a person but a neuter subject—the vision—that is coming soon.

The author now illustrates faith by the example of the heroes of Old Testament history (11:1-40). While commentators point out that the author does not give a definition of faith, he comes closer to a definition than any other New Testament passage. The key words (in the JB translation) are "guarantee" and "proof" (11:1). "Guarantee" touches the objects of hope, and thus is the assurance that God is faithful to his promises. "Proof" does not refer merely to the objects of hope; this would be tautology. The unseen realities are not merely the objects of hope but such things as the plan of God, the will of God to save, the meaning and the value of the saving death of Jesus, the resurrection and exaltation of Jesus. In the course of the chapter, faith is disclosed as fidelity rather than anything else, fidelity to the will of God. Fidelity to God arises from the conviction that God is faithful to his word, that he is able and willing to stand by his pledge. Such fidelity demands a faithful response. Thus, the article of belief in creation (11:3) should not be understood as a truth detached from the truth of the will of God to save it; rather, it supports belief in the power of God to keep his word.

The author speaks at length of the heroes from Abel to Moses, which takes him from Genesis 4 to Exodus 14; then, after a brief allusion to the fall of Jericho (Joshua 6), he sums up the rest of the Old Testament in nine verses (11:32-40). He may have intended a full treatment of the whole of sacred history and then given up when he saw the point which he had reached. One can only praise his decision. Comment on each one is unnecessary.

Enoch elicits a general remark which is somewhat important both for the author's idea of faith and for certain implications in later theology. This is the remark on the necessity of faith (11:6). This verse is most easily understood if faith is understood, as we have suggested, as the human component of the relation of mutual fidelity between man and God; faith demands that one believe that God is true to his word, rewarding those who seek him.

The faith of Noah "convicted" the world (11:7) by showing that God is faithful to his word—both in reward and in punishment. The faith of Abraham, Sarah, Isaac and Jacob (11:8-22) is praised because their confidence in God was maintained without receiving the promise. The author here thinks of Christ as the fulfillment of the promise, and this is a common theme of the New Testament writers. But the book of Genesis was not written by New Testament writers, and in fact the patriarchs are not quite as dependent on faith in the unseen as the author suggests. Abraham, Isaac and Jacob all saw their heirs; and Paul blessed Abraham's faith precisely because he maintained it before he had an heir. They all saw the fulfillment (in the Genesis narratives) of the promise of God's protection and of prosperity in their lands and flocks.

The faith of Moses was the cause of his power (11:23-29). Moses certainly is an apt illustration of one who keeps his eyes on the objects of hope and unseen realities. Yet the author is strangely reticent about the fact that Moses did not live to see the fulfillment of the promise. This might have seemed to raise an objection against his thesis, and possibly he saw this and dealt with the objection by not recognizing it. Similarly he is silent about the lack of faith of the Israelites in the desert and their exclusion from the Promised Land; but he has already touched upon this theme (3:7-19). This would support his thesis; but he would not wish any suggestion that Moses was excluded from the Promised Land for lack of faith.

The other examples of faith (11:32-40) can mostly be

traced in the Old Testament; but some of the examples must have been drawn from the deuterocanonical books (2 Maccabees) and the apocryphal books (Ascension of Isaiah). He repeats his thesis concerning all of these—they maintained their faith without seeing the fulfillment of the promise, which is Christ. Of these heroes this can be stated with less of a strain on the text than his remarks about the patriarchs; the patriarchs may have had their problems, but martyrdom was not among them. The author is a believer in the resurrection, and he does not think that the early heroes had no share in the fulfillment. But compared to the author and his contemporaries, they had to suffer a postponement of the fulfillment.

The JB has given up the classic King James "cloud of witness" (12:1). The author sums up his recital of the heroes of faith by mentioning Jesus, the author and finisher of faith (12:2). He is naively unaware of the difficulties which later theologians would raise; for in orthodox theology Jesus could not have exhibited the virtue of faith. As far as the author of the epistle is concerned, Jesus could have shown faith and did show it; and we may leave to the orthodox theologians the problem of reconciling their doctrine with the belief of the author of the epistle. We can scarcely think of Jesus as experiencing the kind of faith which we experience; yet to think that faith in any degree was impossible for him raises insuperable difficulties with the text of the New Testament. The innermost mind of Jesus does not yield itself to facile analysis.

The words of the author in 12:5-13 certainly allude to the discipline of suffering; as we have already noticed, we cannot identify the situation in the apostolic church to which he speaks. The quotation from Proverbs (12:5-6) is but a sample of many which could be cited from that book to show that the discipline of education is not accomplished without pain. "He who spares the rod hates his son" (Proverbs 13:24), in various forms, has passed into a proverb in many languages. The saying of Aeschylus—"One learns by suffering"—was much used by the late Robert Kennedy. The author had a sufficiency of commonplaces which he might use to express his theme. The author still utters no clear call to martyrdom, which would be somewhat inadequately viewed as a program for self-improvement.

The author then proceeds to a warning against apostasy (12:14-17). He has already dealt with this sin (6:4-6), and we have discussed the problem which his rigor creates. His use of Esau as an example is rather free, but not entirely off the point. Esau is represented in Genesis as the worldling, the man who is governed by the desire of the moment, and in consequence sells his birthright for a snack (Genesis 25:29-34). This is a different account from the one contained in Genesis 27:1-40, which narrates an unvarnished deception of Esau by Rebekah and Jacob. The author conflates the two accounts.

A contrast is established between the old covenant and the new covenant (12:18-29). The author dwells upon the atmosphere of fear and terror in the narratives of the Sinai covenant. No such atmosphere accompanies the revelation of the new covenant. It is not the awesome mountain of Sinai, but the benevolent mountain of Zion, the seat of the chosen city of Jerusalem, which is the scene of the new covenant. The covenant is not revealed in a desolate wilderness; it is witnessed in the presence of the saints, both of the Old Testament and of the New. The mediator is Jesus, contrasted not with Moses but with Abel; the blood of Abel cried for revenge (Genesis 4:10), while the blood of Jesus cries for forgiveness. The author then returns to his favorite theme, the danger of apostasy. If the new covenant is so much more gracious than the old, he implies, so much greater will be the sin of those who are unfaithful to the new covenant. The words of Haggai 2:6 are converted from a promise of salvation to a promise of judgment.

Some moral recommendations follow (13:1-6). They are quite general. The precept of love is specified by an exhortation to hospitality, supported by a reference to the experience of Abraham (Genesis 18:1-15). Christian communities, like Jewish communities scattered through the Mediterranean basin, formed a network of hospitality. The letters of Paul and allusions within the letters show how remarkably well acquainted with each other Christians in different cities were. Similar kindness is to be extended to prisoners; we do not learn that they were imprisoned for their belief. Marital fidelity is commended, and avarice is repudiated, but in conventional terms.

The "leaders" are presented as an example of faith. The heralds of the word of God would appear to be the apostles of the community rather than its chief officers (JB note). These officers are mentioned in 13:17. The author warns against strange doctrines and dietary laws. The allusion to the tabernacle which follows immediately suggests that he is thinking of Jewish Christian doctrines and practices. The altar of the Christians is contrasted with the animal sacrifices of Judaism. This is one more passage in which the author had an opportunity to mention the Eucharist and does not. This strange silence we have noticed before. The altar is not the table of the Eucharist but the cross on which Jesus died. By a midrashic commentary the author compares the ritual of the Day of Atonement, in which the victims were burned outside the camp, to the death of Jesus outside the walls of Jerusalem; the type is fulfilled with every detail. A further thought is suggested by the midrash. Just as Jesus was expelled from the city in his death, so the Christians now live expelled from the human city. The thought is parallel to Philippians 3:20. The uniqueness of the sacrifice of Christ is once again expressed in 13:15; the Christians offer God a sacrifice of praise, which certainly excludes any animal sacrifice and also seems to imply that the author does not think of Christian worship as sacrificial.

Obedience to the officers of the community is recommended (13:17-19); such exhortations are much rarer in the New Testament than they are in contemporary church documents. The responsibility of the officers for the care of souls is a rather strange motive for the exhortation. Ezekiel 3:16-21 (cited in JB margin) commands the prophet to warn the sinner, but absolves him from responsibility if the sinner does not heed the warning. The author declares that he himself has discharged his responsibility.

Commentators generally agree that the conclusion (13:20-25) has suffered some disarrangement. The exhortation and doxology in vv. 20-21 is a sufficient conclusion; it has no marks of the epistolary style, as the beginning of the epistle does not. A common suggestion is that vv. 22-25 were added when a copy of the document was sent to others than those for whom it was written. The conclusion, then, tells us nothing about the place of composition or the original destination. It tells us that the copy came from Italy.

Chapter Twelve
CATHOLIC EPISTLES

The collection of fourteen Pauline epistles (including the epistle to the Hebrews) is followed by a collection of seven epistles called the Catholic Epistles. They have been called by this name since the 2nd century because they have no address to particular churches like the Pauline letters and were considered as addressed to the whole church (Greek *katholike,* whole). Because the term Catholic had become identified with Roman Catholic, many English Protestant translators and commentators since the 16th century have preferred to speak of the General Epistles.

The question of authorship will be briefly treated under each epistle; but the epistles were accepted into the canon of the New Testament on the belief that they were written by apostles. Apostolic authorship was regarded as essential for a canonical book, and this criterion was met if an author like Mark or Luke was thought to be the literary spokesman of an apostle.

The author of the epistle identifies himself as James (Hebrew Jacob), the servant of the Lord. From antiquity this James has been identified with the brother of the Lord, head (not yet bishop) of the church of Jerusalem (Acts 12:17; 15:13; 21:18; 1 Cor 15:7; Gal 2:9, 12). This identification is not made by the author of the epistle. Many critics doubt the identification. Jacob was and is an extremely common Jewish name. The epistle would have to be very early, for James of Jerusalem was killed in 62, according to the Jewish historian Josephus. It is one of the two books of the New Testament (with 1 Peter) written in good Greek style with elements of Greek rhetoric; and it is strange that such Greek would be written by a Galilean villager. The other books of the New Testament show us what to expect from the primitive Jewish Christian group. But many other scholars find these difficulties unconvincing, and the question may be left open; there are not the same difficulties in attributing this epistle to James of Jerusalem as there are in attributing the Pastoral Epistles and Hebrews to Paul.

The epistle is in no sense a letter; it contains nothing personal, lacks the concluding formula of a letter, and its address to the twelve tribes of the dispersion is clearly artificial. The address seems to reflect the early Christian identification of the church with the true Israel. Interpreters regard the work as a treatise written by a Jewish Christian for Jewish Christians. Jesus Christ is mentioned only twice (1:1; 2:1) in passages where the name could easily have been inserted, and there is no reference to the peculiarly Christian beliefs of the redeeming death and baptism. But the literary contacts with other New Testament books are so numerous that no one any longer thinks it is a purely Jewish document accepted by Christians. As a monument of Jewish Christianity it in no way reflects the Judaizing which Paul contested in his letters; it does refer to faith and works (see below), a passage which led Luther to say that the epistle should not have been admitted to the canon.

The literary structure of the epistle is very loose, and it is a collection of sayings on assorted topics, all of them in the area of moral conduct. The literary origins of the epistle really lie in the wisdom books of the Old Testament.

The essays on trials (1:2-12) and temptations (1:13-18) make use in the JB version of a distinction in English which does not exist in Greek, where the same Greek word is employed for both trial and temptation. The distinction is valid, however; James tells his readers to count "trials" as a blessing (1:2), and shortly after tells them not to think that "temptation" comes from God (1:13). One may say that temptation is a trial in which the one tested has been found wanting. No one grows without a challenge; but when one fails the challenge, James has only one explanation: he fails because of his concupiscence (1:14). He pays no attention to such things as bad companions, and leaves no room at all for diabolism.

In an essay on true religion (1:19-27) James insists on the importance of doing the word and not merely hearing it; the word (which must mean the gospel and not the Law) is something which can be done, and in this it is like the Law. The word is a mirror of the ideal man—a slightly contorted figure, for it is a mirror in which one sees not what he is but what he must become. His summary of true religion (1:27) seems impossibly naive, but it was written for naive people. It is made more specific in the following section.

The essay on the poor (2:1-13) atacks discrimination in the church between rich and poor, surely an urgent and contemporary admonition. The theme that God has chosen the poor has echoes in both Old and New Testament (see JB margin). James seems to be addressing a community of the poor, who, one regrets to say, too often fawn upon the rich. Discrimination violates the first commandment, to which James appeals (2:8). The principle that one who breaks one commandment breaks the whole Law is rabbinical, but James applies it to the one commandment of love; if one loves almost all of one's neighbors, one breaks the whole Law.

The essay on faith and works (2:14-26) has been intensely discussed by commentators, but without conclusive results. It could hardly have been written without reference to Paul's thesis about justification by faith; on the other hand, it does not really attack Paul's position, even though James uses Abraham as an example of faith with works, as Paul uses him as an example of justification by faith (Romans 4:1-25; Galatians 3:6-9). But the works which James demands are the works of the commandment of love, not the observance of the Law of Judaism. James here, especially in 2:19, takes faith as assent to a proposition. Paul does not so understand it.

The essay on control of the tongue (3:1-12) uses a great many figures of speech; this leads commentators to think that James made use of some rhetorical commonplaces from profane literature. Faults of speech, according to James, are the most difficult to control; in this he agrees with much Old Testament wisdom, where indiscreet speech is the token which reveals the fool.

An essay on true and false wisdom (3:13-18) makes wise conduct the test of the wise man. The work of wisdom is reconciliation; the passage has a number of echoes in the Gospel (see JB margin). Commentators believe that both the Gospels and the epistle drew from a store of Christian "wisdom" teaching of the primitive church.

An essay on unity (4:1-12) earnestly rebukes quarrels within the Christian community, a theme to which Paul spoke several times (see JB margin). These were not disputes about doctrine and conduct, but the vulgar quarrels of those who seek their own way. Such an attitude is friendliness with the world (4:4); but withdrawal from the world is one of the components of true religion (1:27).

A warning to the rich (4:13—5:6) is addressed in the first place to merchants. In the ancient world most merchants were actually traveling peddlers; the risks of merchandising were great. James sees in the risks the impending judgment of God which the merchants challenge. His sharpest words are addressed to those who hold back the wages of the workers; casual labor was paid by the day, for the laborer had no margin to carry him beyond the day. In addition James contrasts the luxury of the rich with the destitute condition of the poor. This sharp contrast of extremes was characteristic of ancient society, but it is disapproved both by the prophets of the Old Testament and by the gospel.

The conclusion (5:7-20) contains assorted recommendations. James refers to the Parousia (5:9), one of the indications of the Christian origin of the epistle. On the other hand, his examples of virtue are drawn from the Old Testament. The anointing of the sick (5:14-15) has for hundreds of years been taken as evidence of the sacrament of Extreme Unction. James goes from this rite to the efficacy of prayer. Commentators have remarked that 5:17-18 is the only biblical justification for prayer for favorable weather.

First Epistle of Peter

This epistle, like the epistle of James, is not a letter, even though it has an address and a conclusion. The author clearly identifies himself as Peter, although he was written through Silvanus (see below). The place of writing is Babylon (5:13); but no one doubts that this is a code word for Rome. The authorship of Peter is questioned by many critics. Like the epistle of James, it is written in some of the best Greek of the New Testament. This can be explained by attributing the composition to Silvanus. This is almost surely the same person as Silas, the companion of Paul (Acts 15-18), and mentioned as Silvanus in 1 Th 1:1; 2 Th 1:1; 2 Cor 1:19. Like many Jews, he had both a Jewish and a Greek (in this case Latin) name. This supposes somewhat gratuitously that Silas was able to write stylish Greek with rhetorical flourishes. If Peter was the author it must be placed no later than 64. As for James, the question must be left open. The address is somewhat artificial, and uses the names of regions rather than the proper Roman provincial names.

A more serious argument against the Peter-Silvanus authorship is a rather apparent lack of unity; almost all critics find a break at 4:11-12 (notice the doxology), and identify 1:3—4:11 as a homily composed for candidates for baptism. In this case the original letter, if there was one, contained only the exhortations of 4:12—5:14; but even here there is a somewhat disorganized collection. It is no credit either to Peter or to Silvanus to attribute to them such a pastiche.

The baptismal homily begins with the theme of the Christian salvation (1:3-9), which is a new birth with the resurrection of Christ; the theme of the new birth is found also in Paul and John. This new life looks to fulfillment in the eschatological age. Whatever sufferings the believer must endure before the end of time are simply tests "for a short time" (1:6). This view appears to show no awareness of persecutions like that of Nero in Rome or, for those who think the epistle has a later date, the persecution in the latter years of Domitian (A.D. 96). This is the salvation which the prophets foretold; from the very beginnings of the church Christians found a Christological interpretation of the prophetic books.

Salvation leads to an appeal to holiness (1:13-21), couched in quite general terms. Holiness in the Old Testament was a condition of ritual purity by which one was rendered fit to partake in the cult. This condition in the baptized is created by the atoning blood of Jesus; the theme of the atoning and purifying blood of Jesus appears in Hebrews 9:1--10:18. The major fruit of holiness is love, the new commandment (1:22-25). As newborn infants the baptized should desire nothing but milk; but the author uses the figure in a quite different sense from 1 Cor 3:2, where milk is the food of the immature. Here it is the food of nature, pure and unadulterated; by an obscure phrase which translators stumble over he probably designates milk as "the word," the gospel.

The theme of the new temple and the priesthood (2:4-10) is analogous to Paul's theme of the body of Christ; and Paul also uses the building image with reference to the body (Ephesians 2:20-22). The Christians are the true Israel and the true priesthood. By applying to all the designations of temple and priesthood the author rejects the category of the sacred as it was known in Judaism.

The author now turns to various duties which flow from holiness. The first of these is a general obligation to present good works before unbelievers (2:11-12); the charges of various crimes against Christians ran through most of the history of the early church, and the author wishes Christians to furnish no ground for these. Next he proposes obedience to civil authority (2:13-17); there seems to be no expectation that civil authority would prohibit the profession of the Christian faith. Strangely in this exhortation to obedience the author introduces the theme of freedom; this must be freedom in the Pauline sense, and even more, for it implies that no human authority has the power to constrain the Christian.

Instructions for slaves (2:18-24), we have seen, rub the modern Christian the wrong way, especially when the author makes no distinction between the kind and the unfair owners. Presenting Christ as an example of submissiveness before unfair treatment probably meant no more in the first century than it does now. The modern Christian is usually sure that however one is to deal with the inhumanity of man to man, one must not bear it as Jesus bore it. The modern Christian sees no redemptive value in such suffering.

Instructions for marriage (3:1-7), like similar instructions in the Pauline epistles, emphasize obedience in the wife and kindness in the husband. We have already adverted to the cultural pattern implicit in these instructions. The author is more rigorous than any other New Testament writer in speaking of feminine dress and cosmetics, although no more rigorous than Isaiah 3:16-24. Some study of the stylish Roman lady, if space permitted, would help furnish background for this puritanism, and perhaps make us wonder why other New Testament writers are so casual on the subject. The curious reader may look up the sixth Satire of Juvenal, a quite pagan Roman poet of the 2nd century A.D.

The Christian community should be a community of love (3:8-12). This is clear enough; it should be pointed out, however, that it is not a community closed in on itself, hostile to the outside world. The admonitions for persecution (3:13-17) again do not seem to reflect the massive attacks of the Roman government in later centuries, or even such mob action as Nero encouraged in Rome. Rather, they seem to refer to the petty harassment of hostile neighbors. The author thought it important that Christians should be able to give an account of their belief and their life; and he creates the masterful aphorism of 3:17.

Christ is the example of the Christian compelled to suffer and to risk martyrdom (3:18—4:6). Interpreters agree only that the passage is difficult and they propose various interpretations, none of which is satisfactory. The proclamation to the spirits in prison (3:19) and to the dead (4:6) presupposes a naive belief in the existence of souls in Sheol and possibly in the imprisonment of the fallen angels described in the apocryphal book of Enoch. The proclamation of the victory of the risen Christ does not imply for such an opportunity to believe; the author's meaning is that there is no corner of the universe in which the victory of Christ is not known. This victory empowers Christians to rise above the level of pagan life; they share his victory, and they should not fall so that they must be submitted to his judgment.

The homily concludes with an exhortation to Christian love (4:7-11). This exhortation is specified by a recommendation that the love of each take the form which is suitable to his own charisma. The author here echoes Paul (see 1 Cor 12:4-11); Christian love is not a vague and formless attitude. It becomes practical and meaningful when each one realizes that kind of service which God has empowered him to render within the community. We have noticed above that the doxology (4:11) suggests a concluding formula.

The following exhortation to fidelity in suffering (4:12-19) comes in abruptly unless we think that the baptismal homily originally was not connected with the exhortation. Again we notice that there is no suggestion of a massive official persecution of Christians. The lesson of 3:17 is resumed; if one might be persecuted, it is important that one be persecuted for the right reason. Only if one suffers simply for being a Christian can one think of suffering as a share in the passion of Christ.

Instructions to the elders (5:1-4) raise questions which have been discussed in earlier epistles about the officers of the primitive Christian churches; this passage adds no new information. The author calls himself simply an elder (rather surprising, since he calls himself an apostle in 1:1). The office of elder is also the office of shepherd, an ancient Near Eastern metaphor for king found also in the Old Testament, and applied by Jesus to himself (John 10) and to Peter (John 21:15-17). The author does not seem to know this passage. He warns against avarice and bullying in the elders.

The author instructs the rest of the church (5:5-11) to be obedient to the elders. He seems to anticipate a more vigorous persecution than they have yet known. In any hypothesis of the date of the epistle this forecast was quite correct. "The enemy" (5:8) is more likely to be identified with the persecutors than with an extraterrestrial evil being. The author comforts the believers with the assurance that the time is short; the impending Parousia will stop the persecution and vindicate the believers. The assurance is greater than faith in the Parousia warrants; and this author actually creates a greater difficulty than Paul created with his belief in early Parousia. Deliverance from the Roman persecutors through an early Parousia was a nonreality.

Three Epistles of John

The First Epistle of John lacks entirely the epistolary formulae of address and conclusion, and contains no reference to persons and places. It is more properly a homily or a tract rather than an epistle. This does not mean that it was written without reference to a particular church or a particular situation; but we cannot identify either the church or the situation. Both 2 and 3 John, on the contrary, have addresses. "The Lady, the chosen one" is understood to mean a church, not a person. 3 John is addressed to Gaius, a member of the church (and possibly an officer) with whose problems the letter is concerned. No name of the church is given, and the brevity of the letters does not tell us much about the occasion of their writing.

The author identifies himself as "the Elder" in 2-3 John. Modern critics agree generally that the Johannine writings (except the Apocalypse) are to be treated as a literary group, at least in the sense that they proceed from a single school. 1 John has more literary affinities with the Gospel of John than it has with any other book. 2-3 John, too brief to permit very certain conclusions, can come from the author of 1 John. The differences between the Gospel and 1 John permit one to suggest a school, although many critics remark that the differences are no greater than one finds in the works of a single writer at different periods of his career. Critics generally believe that 1 John was written before the Gospel.

The question of whether John the Elder is John the son of Zebedee, one of the Twelve, was discussed in our treatment of the Fourth Gospel. There we noted that the majority of critical opinion, for good if not absolutely convincing reasons, doubts the traditional identification of the author. The epistles add nothing to the question. The author of 1 John is not named. The author of 2-3 John is the Elder; we have noticed in connection with 1 Peter 5:1 that it is somewhat strange that an apostle should use the title of elder. But most interpreters think that "the Elder" of 2-3 John does not indicate a church office but a personal appellative. Some interpreters call him "the Ancient" (which suggests a translation of the Greek word into French rather than English). One is driven to such paraphrases as "the Senior" or even, more colloquially, "the Old Man." In any case, we still wonder why an apostle would not use the title of apostle; and this was recognized even by some ancient Christian scholars, who distinguished between John the Apostle and John the Elder.

Commentators despair of outlining the thought of 1 John, which is most kindly described as rambling. One modern commentator speaks of three successive waves of thought; we may add that he means three successive waves of the same thoughts. The style of 1 John is not only rambling, it is monotonous. The use of sense lines in the JB version is an effort to disguise the basic monotony of the style.

In the introduction (1:1-3) the author identifies himself as eyewitness of the saving event, the manifestation of the Word. It becomes clear later in the epistle that he emphasizes the reality of the incarnation; it was truly the Word and not merely an apparition of some kind which he witnessed. The affirmation can be compared with the prologue of the Gospel of John (1:1-14).

That God is light (1:5-7) is not only a theme of the Fourth Gospel, but a theme of the Old Testament and of ancient Near Eastern religions, in which light is the element of the creator deity. Here light is identified with truth, another theme of the Fourth Gospel. Sin, of course, is opposed to the light and the truth (1:8--2:2); the author does not expect perfect freedom from sin even in the regenerate. The author probably admits, in common with other New Testament writers, that there is a limit beyond which forgiveness is possible through Christ. That Christ is a sacrificial victim (2:1) is not a theme of the Fourth Gospel. The title advocate (paraclete"), applied here to Jesus, is a title of the Spirit in John 14:26; 15:25; 16:7.

John, like James, is a theologian of works; and the work which he proposes is the same work which Paul proposes. He speaks of the commandments, but he is thinking of only one commandment, the commandment which includes all the others. This is the assurance that one remains in the light and truth. He plays on the words "old" and "new" somewhat pedantically; the commandment is old, because it is the original message of Jesus; it is new because it is revolutionary, the commandment which brings light to the world.

Opposition to the world (2:12-17) is also a theme of the Fourth Gospel; the Johannine writings characteristically speak of "the world" as a reality hostile to God and to Christ. The somewhat painful enumeration of those addressed as fathers, young men and children seems to have no particular reference to age or condition; it is merely a rhetorical device. The readers, it is supposed, already know the Johannine meaning of "the world." The author creates a somewhat pregnant phrase for the world in 2:16, long rendered in the older English versions as "the concupiscence of the flesh, the concupiscence of the eyes and the pride of life," doubtfully improved in the JB. In terms of the classic seven vices, the phrase designates lust, avarice and pride.

The Antichrist (2:18-29) is a word found only in 1-2 John. The word does not designate a single person or a single institution; the present passage makes it clear that the Antichrist is a type of person, and in fact antichristian would be a more accurate description in our terms. The author speaks of members of the Christian community who are now recognized as never having been genuine members. But the Antichrists do not appear to have withdrawn from the Christian community; they are still in a position to mislead those to whom the document is written (2:26). The appearance of the Antichrists is a phenomenon of the last days; and we have noticed in discussing the Fourth Gospel that this Gospel seems to know no eschatology of the Parousia. This is one of the most striking differences between 1 John and the Gospel.

The Antichrists deny that Jesus is the Christ (the Messiah). This obscure phrase, in the opinion of most interpreters, indicates an early heresy which denied that Jesus was the Word. The Word dwelt in Jesus, or appeared in Jesus, but was a different reality which was not born, and did not die and rise. An early Christological heresy was the doctrine called Docetism, which taught that the man Jesus was simply an optical illusion in which the Word appeared. The author does not clearly mean this heresy, and possibly he was not deeply interested in stating erroneous beliefs accurately.

Somewhat abruptly the author turns to the theme of God's love of man (3:1-2). This is the transforming love which makes men children of God and assimilates them to the Father, a likeness which is fulfilled only in the eschatological vision. The conditions by which the process of assimilation is to be accomplished are set forth in the verses which follow.

The first step is to break with sin (3:3-9). In 1:8--2:2 the author admits that the victory of the believer over sin is less than total. Here, however, he appears to demand that it be total. Like other New Testament writers on this topic, he is not perfectly consistent; and efforts of some interpreters to rescue him conclude with such paraphrases as this: The Christian is free from sin except when he sins. Certainly the ideal and the objective of the saving act is victory over sin; Christian doctrine generally treats this as a part of the eschatological fulfillment.

The second step is the observance of the commandments, and again there is only one commandment. One sees how this wave of thought repeats the first wave. The new element is the antithesis between God and the devil, a theme of the Fourth Gospel. Nevertheless, the theme has its new development. Perhaps nowhere else in the Bible is lack of love so clearly identified with murder; it is suggested in Matthew 5:21-16. And since hatred is murder, by association the writer goes on to assert that love is the giving of one's life. Of this, Jesus is example. More likely than the demand of one's life is the demand of one's goods for the needy; and the author again becomes a theologian of works, the test of the genuinity of love. This is turn gives the believer confidence to approach God. The author vastly simplifies Christianity in 3:23. The fruit of observance of the commandment is the indwelling (3:24), a Johannine theme; the author does not make use of the Pauline themes of the body or of the building, in line with his somewhat noninstitutional church.

Faith of itself is no assurance; it must be protected by vigilance against false teaching (4:1-6). It is difficult to reconstruct a theology of the "spirits" according to this author; but the Old Testament in its early books knew good and evil spirits, and one hardly need go beyond this. The Qumran writings also make the distinction, and may associate this theme in John with the Qumran group. The Christological heresy rejected here is the same heresy rejected above—viz., that the Word did not really become flesh. This is the teaching of the false spirits and the false prophets. These are the people of the "world," even though they are Christians; they have joined the hostile cosmic host.

The author returns to his main theme, love, at even greater length (4:7-21). Fraternal love is rooted in the love of God for man, the love revealed in the Son. The author makes his celebrated identification of God with love, by which he certainly does not mean to reduce a personal reality to an abstraction. A rhetorical emphasis is achieved when he says "God is love" rather than "God loves." This is the personal act which sums up God's personal reality and dominates all the other aspects under which he is revealed. It is rather paradoxical when he concludes from God's love of us not that we should love God but that we should love each other (4:11); but the paradox is deliberate, and it is clarified in the exposition which follows.

Before he gets to this point, however, he makes another paradoxical statement concerning the incompatibility of love and fear (4:17-18). This statement has caused anguish to many theologians. The paradox of the statement is not in the terms themselves but in the simple fact that such perfect love is rarely if ever found in the Christian experience; we hesitate to admit that Christian love of man for God is generally imperfect. Now the first paradox is clarified; man does not see God, he has no immediate experience of God. He can love God immediately only by loving his brother, and his claim to love God directly without going through his brothers is a lie. Once again, this is the only commandment.

The author then returns to the theme of faith (5:5-12). The object of faith is the Incarnate Son of God, the same object which he has proposed above. Here he emphasizes the reality of the death of Jesus; the reference to water and blood echoes John 19:34, and critics suppose that the Johannine tradition was older than the Gospel of John. The threefold witness endures in the church; the charismatic Spirit, the water of baptism, and the redeeming death reenacted in the Eucharist. The conclusion (5:13) joins the themes of faith in the Son and eternal life.

The JB calls 5:14-21 a postscript. Its themes are the power of prayer and the sure victory of God over sin; once again the author is somewhat ambiguous concerning the completeness of the Christian's victory over sin, and he admits the possibility of a sin which is not "deadly," from which theology has formed the distinction of mortal and venial sin.

2-3 John are so light in content that nothing but apostolic authorship could have gotten them into the canon. Yet we have seen that the authorship of John the Apostle is highly doubtful. When we say that the contents are light, we do not mean that the contents are trivial; they are substantially important. But they are the same topics treated at greater length in 1 John, and 2 John adds nothing to this treatment. The first of these is the commandment of love. The second is the Christological heresy; and here the terms used by the author do suggest the heresy of Docetism, which denied the reality of the body of Jesus.

We remarked above that the author was not deeply concerned with stating erroneous beliefs accurately. The author goes beyond the earlier books of the New Testament in denying association or even a greeting, the elementary sign of civility, to those who teach false doctrine. The author evidently has no hope of rescuing the brother from his error, and a real fear that he will succeed in spreading the error. False doctrine is for him a "sin unto death" (I Jn 5:16).

3 John is not concerned with doctrine but with a dispute which we can scarcely reconstruct. Gaius is a member of the church in which Diotrephes wields authority. It is impossible to define the office or the scope of the authority which Diotrephes held; but the author does not deny the authority of Diotrephes. Presumably Gaius also had some authority, and one is tempted to say that both were "overseers" or "elders." The relation of the author, the Elder, to the church is undefined. There is really no evidence that he was its founder, as in the case of Paul who was the founder of the churches to which he wrote. He makes no claim to the possession of apostolic authority. Diotrephes successfully refuses to receive either his letters or his personal representatives, and the author has no recourse except to enter his complaints in a personal visit to the church. This is rather feeble compared to Paul's response to the Corinthians.

The author praises the hospitality of Gaius to visiting brothers, and recommends Demetrius, who may have been the bearer of the letter. This is probably more than graciousness; the brothers were apparently embarking on missionary journeys to places still unevangelized. These may have been the ones whom Diotrephes rejected; and we may have an early instance of a jurisdictional dispute.

Epistles of Jude and Peter

Both these epistles have a very general address and are directed to no particular situation which we can recognize. 2 Peter clearly claims apostolic authority derived from the authorship of Peter. The same apostolic authority was no doubt attributed to Jude, for early Christians reckoned that apostolic authority was necessary for a canonical book. But the epistle itself may be less clear in claiming apostolic authorship than the early Christians thought. Jude claims to be the brother of James; no doubt this means the Jude who is named as "a brother of the Lord" in Matthew 13:55; Mark 6:3. Jude is also found in the lists of the Twelve in Luke 6:16; Acts 1:13. Instead of Jude, Thaddaeus appears in the lists of

Matthew 10:3; Mark 3:18. Modern scholars generally doubt the identity of Jude of the Twelve and Jude the kinsman of the Lord; this would imply that the epistle, if written by Jude, is not the work of an apostle. Perhaps the best reason for supporting the authorship by Jude is that Jude is otherwise so little known that we do not know why anyone should claim his name. This is not convincing. Critics, however, generally deny that Peter wrote 2 Peter, either himself or through another. It is often called the latest writing of the New Testament, as late as the second century A.D. If this judgment is correct, it is impossible that it should come from Peter who, according to tradition, was killed in the reign of Nero (A.D. 68).

Not only do the two epistles treat the same topics; there is evidence that the author of 2 Peter made use of the epistle of Jude. The reader can compare Jude 4-13 with 2 Peter 2:1-18 and Jude 17-18 with 2 Peter 3:1-3. Critics generally agree that Jude is the model of 2 Peter and not the reverse. This relationship does not afford indications of the date of either epistle; Jude, while earlier than 2 Peter, is one ot the latest books of the New Testament. Both epistles have that concern for true and false doctrine which we have found elsewhere in late books. The character of the false doctrine cannot be determined with certainty.

The purpose of the introduction (1:1-2) seems to be rather to affirm the authorship of Peter than to give direction to the epistle. There follows a brief description of the Christian life which is somewhat distinctive in the New Testament. The author shares with the Johannine writings the idea of the Christian life as the knowledge of God. The idea of "sharing the divine nature" (1:4), however, is not found elsewhere in the Bible and is derived from the language of the Hellenistic religious world. The climactic catalogue of virtues (1:5-7) is a Greek figure of speech; the virtues, however, are peculiarly Christian and include the Christian virtue of love as climactic. The author emphasizes the importance of his message by affirming his personal witness (1:12-18); in the common interpretation this assumption of the person of Peter is fictitious. Evidence of the Parousia was had by those who witnessed the tranfiguration, in which the glory of the risen Lord was momentarily revealed. They saw the figure, so to speak. This is the significance of the transfiguration in the synoptic Gospels; and if the date of 2 Peter is as late as many think, the author could have had the Gospel narratives of the transfiguration. The transfiguration is also a confirmation of prophecy (1:19-21). We have elsewhere alluded to the somewhat free Christological interpretation of prophecy which the early church devised. Here, however, the author introduces a new element into interpretation; he denies the right of "private interpretation." He does not affirm that interpretation belongs to the church (and to the authority in the church) except by implication. His principle is that as the writing of prophecy was charismatic, so its interpretation must be charismatic. The Spirit who inspired the writers must also inspire those who declare the meaning of the writings.

The author then launches into an attack on false teachers (2:1-10). We have noticed that he gives no indication of what the false doctrines are; he is much more interested in the certainty of the punishment which God will inflict upon them. Regretfully he admits that they will deceive many. The certainty of judgment is illustrated by examples both from the sacred books and from apocryphal literature. The angels who sinned are the "sons of God" of Genesis 6:1-4; but their punishment is derived from the apocryphal books of Enoch. Other examples are the deluge and the destruction of Sodom; but the author rambles somewhat in making these examples not only of judgment on the wicked but of deliverance of the righteous who were dangerously close to the judgment. Noah as "the preacher of righteousness" is contrasted with the false teachers; and Lot is the model of the devout Christian who is shocked by the shameless behavior of the heathen. Such need not fear the judgment which the author announces against the false teachers.

The author, after being briefly distracted by the theme of deliverance, returns to his charge against the false teachers (2:10-22); it is obvious that this is a theme which he enjoys more. In fact his invective is so comprehensive that it loses its effectiveness. The false teachers have all the vices, especially the gross vices of gluttony and lust. The author uses the abusive language of animal imagery. Perhaps the only clues to the errors of the false teachers is the allusion to their promise of freedom (2:19). This could well refer to a variety of Gnosticism which taught that baptism not only liberated the Christian from the Law but from all moral obligation. Literally the Christian could do whatever he pleased without sin. If this were the error attacked, one can more easily understand the author's use of rather gross animal imagery. The author is especially indignant at the relapse of those who have believed; one may compare Hebrews 6:4-8. The animal imagery reaches its peak (or its depth) in the two proverbs, the first from Prov 26:11 and the second from the Jewish Book of Ahikar. Dogs were generally despised in the Near East, and swine were offensive to Jews.

It is an easy transition from judgment to Parousia, and the same question could be asked about each: What is the delay? The author attests that the question was asked. There is no longer any thought of an imminent Parousia, which we have seen in the early epistles of Paul and in some passages of the Gospels. The question about the delay of the Parousia is one of the indications that the epistle is later than the life of Peter. Yet the author rather solemnly begins his discussion (3:1-10) with another affirmation that he is Peter. Here he shows that he knew 1 Peter. As we have remarked above, his fictitious identity has nothing to do with his conviction of the truth which he speaks.

His words suggest that the delay of the Parousia was the occasion of shipwreck of the faith for some Christians. If this is true, we must note that it was not the last time in the history of the church that its members have been disappointed and perhaps disillusioned because they believed in things which were not true. An expectation that God will intervene in history according to the desires of those who believe in him can be found in ancient Israel as well as in early Christianity. It has survived into more recent Christianity. If God does not act according to the schedule we have set for him, then he loses all claim upon our faith. The answer of the author is not entirely complete and not entirely appropriate; but it is an effort to respond to a serious and genuine problem.

The first part of his answer is not wholly felicitous. The biblical tradition of the deluge includes a promise that God will not again destroy the world by water (Genesis 9:11-16). The author, respecting this text, announces that the world will end not by water but by fire. He sees no other way in which a cosmic judgment can be fulfilled; and he is compelled to accept the necessity of a cosmic judgment. Not all biblical writers were impelled by this necessity, although some kind of collapse of the visible universe was a common feature of late biblical and Jewish apocalyptic literature. Belief in judgment took extreme forms in such imagery. Commentators point out that, in the entire Bible, a universal conflagration is seen only here; the idea, however, appeared in other beliefs, especially in Persian religion. Commentators also point out that here we are dealing with imagery in which the belief in world judgment is expressed, and in no sense with a literal prediction of the process by which judgment will be accomplished.

The author deals with the delay of the Parousia by introducing a difference between God's time and man's time. We should not apply to God our own sense of urgency. The author introduces the theme of the patience of God with human iniquity. The explanation is not entirely satisfactory, but then no explanation is. It is a common biblical theme in both Old and New Testaments that man must await the acts of God, and even that it could be dangerous to wish for them.

The conclusion (3:11-18) makes practical applications: One must live in such a way that one is ready for the great judgment. The conflagration is to be followed by the creation of a "new heavens and a new earth" (Isaiah 66:22). The author, still posing as Peter, warns against misunderstanding the letters of Paul. This certainly presupposes a collection of Paul's epistles, but we cannot determine how many epistles the collection included. He suggests in 3:16 that these epistles have achieved a rank approaching that of "sacred scripture"—a hypothesis which seems unlikely even at the latest possible date for 2 Peter. Obviously he does not wish to dispute either the authority or the content of the Pauline epistles. No less obviously the history of theology affords abundant examples of those who have distorted the meaning of Paul's epistles. The author may mean precisely those parts of the Pauline epistles which exhibit a belief in an imminent Parousia. If this is what he meant, it is only fair to say that these passages still cause difficulty for interpreters.

Jude

The introduction (1-2), as we have remarked, is general. The immediate occasion of the letter is the appearance of false teachers (3-4). Like the author of 2 Peter, the author does not identify the false doctrines. The brief description he gives suggests the error of complete moral liberty and the denial of the reality of the incarnation: We have noticed these errors in the epistles of John and 2 Peter. He adduces examples of the punishment God has inflicted on unbelief (5-7). The first of these (not employed in 2 Peter, which depends on this passage) is the unbelief of Israel in the desert. Then the author refers to the sin of the angels (Genesis 6:1-4) and the sin of Sodom (Genesis 19). The author links these two examples by a theme not used by the author of 2 Peter: The sin of the angels was commerce with human females, and the sin of Sodom was attempted sexual commerce with angels, for the guests of Lot are represented as angels. This to the author is the height of unnatural vice. The punishment of the angels, as we noted in treating 2 Peter, is found not in the Bible but in the books of Enoch.

The false teachers, in addition to other sins, show disrespect for the angels (8-20). A quotation from the apocryphal book *The Assumption of Moses* shows that even the archangel Michael showed respect for the devil, a fallen angel. He uses imagery as the author of 2 Peter did. The false teachers are compared to famous biblical villains—Cain, Balaam and Korah; the last two can be considered as false teachers, although it is difficult to include Cain in this category. The author applies to them a prophecy found in the apocryphal books of Enoch. The faithful have been warned against false teachers; there are many passages in the epistles, especially the later epistles, which he could have had in mind (17-19). False teachers, as in the other epistles, are forerunners of the eschatological event. In this feature the belief in an imminent Parousia survives; the Christians of the apostolic age did not conceive a church that would live habitually with error, not only in those outside but even within her own membership. It deserves notice that no other biblical writer quotes three apocryphal texts in one paragraph.

The application for the readers (20-23) is a cautious admonition to charity toward the misguided. The author is as aware of the danger for the faithful in dealing with the misguided as he is of the spiritual needs of the misguided. He is less rigorous than the author of 2 Peter; but the believers in error are primarily a menace to the true believers, not an object of their charity. Here again we can see the belief that baptism was, so to speak, a single chance. There was no recovery from relapse into unbelief. The epistle concludes with a conventional doxology (24-25).

Conclusion

The reader may conclude his reading of the Catholic Epistles with a feeling that in these writings the New Testament is turning toward trivia. This suspicion may have been rising in his mind as he read the Pastoral Epistles. If he is a student of theology, he will have noticed that the Catholic Epistles are not quoted and studied with anything like the attention which is given to the great Pauline epistles. There are some strange features of belief in the Catholic Epistles which we have made no attempt to conceal or gloss over in these remarks. The careful reader of the New Testament will never feel quite at home in the apostolic church; but the discomfort which he feels in the Catholic Epistles is different from the discomfort he feels in the Pauline epistles. Paul, he fears, makes demands on him which the modern church does not make, and which he fears he would not meet if they were made. The Catholic Epistles, on the other hand, reveal certain limitations which he knows quite well and with which he is uneasy. For example, the warnings of the Catholic Epistles to have no communion with those who believe false doctrine may offend not only his ecumenical principles but even his sense of common decency. How, he may wonder, can one reconcile this exclusiveness with the teaching of the commandment of love which the Catholic Epistles preserve?

There has long been a feeling among believers that the Bible, which is inspired by God, should always reach the highest level of thought and style; what else is worthy of God? The biblical student soon learns that the inspired writers are no better, as a collection of human beings and writers, than any other collection of men. There are large portions of the books of the Old Testament which are narrow-minded and dull. The student learns that inspiration means that God used what he had available. The evidence of the books is that great intellectual and literary talent was not always available. One may, for the sake of comparison, ask what kind of sacred books would be written if God had no other talent available except that talent which writes modern advertising. It would be dreadful in quality and entirely shallow, but it would still be the inspired word of God. It would probably not reach the level of the Catholic Epistles.

My purpose in these remarks is to warn against the kind of Bible worship which belief in the inspired text has often produced in both Jews and Christians. At its worst this belief has made the Bible a substitute for God. A parallel aberration has made the church a substitute for God. Both Bible and church are means through which man reaches God. Both Bible and church are at times clearly human, so human as to be depressing. At their worst they are still the place of encounter with the God who has revealed himself in sundry places and in diverse manners, even when in them God is perceived as through a glass, darkly. In the Catholic Epistles one can see the beginnings of that narrowness which has so often been characteristic of the church, the readiness to consign all lost sheep to hell in a handbasket. It is other books of the New Testament which enable us to put this attitude of the Catholic Epistles in proper perspective—that is to say, to recognize it as narrow and intolerant. To borrow a phrase from the Catholic Epistles, it is not only the epistles of our brother Paul that the unlearned and the unstable wrest to their own destruction.

If we consider the Scriptures as a record of the encounter of man with God, we must leave room for the small and the narrow as well as the great. We can find echoes of ourselves in the petty and narrow elements. We see a vision of our potentialities in those books which make demands upon us beyond our expectations and powers.